CONCISE CAMPAIGNS

General Editor: R. L. V. ffrench Blake

1

THE CRIMEAN WAR

R. L. V. FFRENCH BLAKE

LEO COOPER · LONDON

First published in Great Britain by
LEO COOPER LTD.
196 Shaftesbury Avenue
London WC2
© *Copyright R. L. V. ffrench Blake 1971*

ISBN 0 85052 084 3

Printed in Great Britain by
Ebenezer Baylis & Son Limited
The Trinity Press, Worcester, and London

CONTENTS

ACKNOWLEDGEMENTS

I should like to express my gratitude to the following persons or organizations:

Patrick Perry for valuable historical advice; the staffs of the libraries at the Ministry of Defence, the Admiralty, and the Staff College; the members of the photo-reproduction department at the School of Military Survey; Major Bartelot of the Royal Artillery Institution at Woolwich; Mrs Handby for rapid and efficient typing; and Patrick Leeson, who drew the maps.

ILLUSTRATIONS

Between pages 86 and 87

MAPS

INTRODUCTION

This book, the first of a series of Concise Guides to various campaigns, was born out of the frustration experienced in trying to write a short chapter on the Crimean War in a regimental history. My intention was to sketch a brief general outline of the campaign, and then to fill in the detail of the part played by my regiment. A visit to the War Office Library revealed some twenty-four square feet of books on the Crimean War—headed by Kinglake's eight volumes; yet Kinglake ends with the death of Lord Raglan, with ten months of war still ahead. E. H. Nolan's eight-volume work proved to be an indigestible mass of detail, but was the first indication to me of the full scope of the war, since it includes accounts of the Danube War, Asia Minor and the naval campaigns in the Baltic and Pacific. Generals Hamley and MacMunn both give excellent short accounts, but concentrate on the Crimea, largely from the British point of view. Woodham-Smith and Hibbert deal with special subjects, Russell is too much the journalist; a legion of eye-witnesses give their own limited views—in short, I felt the need for a small guide to the whole war, and this book is the result.

It is of necessity full of imperfections—it is impossible to mention everything that ought to be included, for economic reasons of space and price alone. I have adopted a makeshift spelling of Russian names, based on the usage in *Encyclopaedia Britannica*, and using the principle of economy in spelling— thus Menshikov rather than Mentschikoff, Burliuk for Bourliouk, as in older histories. The old Danubian place names have been used, but their modern equivalents have been given where possible.

I have included among the appendices a complete key to the British cavalry and infantry regiments with their titles in 1854, 1900 and 1971, which I hope will be of help to students of regimental matters. The bibliography contains some comment on what the student may expect to find in the works mentioned.

No writer has produced better maps than Kinglake, whose work nearly all other authors have copied; but with the passage of time, plans have become distorted, roads and tracks have been included which never existed, and other features have been falsified. There is a fine set of Crimean maps in the Staff College Library, surveyed by a Royal Engineer team in 1856, and containing every detail of the Sevastopol area. A photostat of these maps is to be seen in the 17th/21st Lancers Museum at Belvoir Castle. One of the set is reproduced on pages 120 and 121 of this work. The maps of the Crimea in this book, admirably drawn by Patrick Leeson, are based on this same set.

For illustrations, I have leant heavily upon the well-known engravings from the drawings by William Simpson. Comparison of these drawings with contemporary photographs shows them to be on the whole very accurate topographically. I have therefore studied them with a new eye, looking into the backgrounds rather than at the main subjects, and identifying features from the map. Brackenbury's *Campaign in the Crimea* (2 volumes) gives detailed descriptions of this whole series of prints, which incidentally, can still be bought comparatively cheaply.

The student will not find everything here, but I hope that he may be helped on the way to further research and exploration.

Midgham Park Farm   R. L. V. FFRENCH BLAKE
Woolhampton
1971

CHAPTER I

Events Leading to the War

The name of the Crimean War has done much to obscure its true character. The land front stretched from the Iron Gates on the Danube to the foothills of the Caucasus mountains; the naval war reached round half the world. British historians, led by Kinglake, whose account ends with the death of Lord Raglan, tend to ignore operations outside the Crimea, because there were no British forces involved, other than a handful of officers advising and leading Turkish troops.

The main cause of the war was Russia's desire for territorial expansion, particularly towards a port in the Mediterranean. The immediate excuses for war were more complicated, but of a pattern familiar enough today—the 'protection of oppressed minorities' in the target country, and reprisals for the death of nationals in religious riots. The apparently inevitable drift into war was aggravated by the intransigent nature of the rulers of the opposing countries, and by bad diplomacy.

The war on land was fought in three main theatres—the Danube, Asia Minor, and the Crimea. A Russian invasion of the Danube provinces was defeated and totally repulsed by the Turkish army; a similar attack in Asia Minor was held with difficulty by local forces under British commanders, assisted by guerrilla action in the Caucasus. The invasion of the Crimea represented a counter-thrust by the Allies, designed to bring Russia to heel by the destruction of her principal naval base, Sevastopol. Success came too late, at a cost as great to the victors as to the defeated.

1

The naval war was conducted in the Black Sea, the Sea of Azov, the Baltic, the White Sea, and on the Pacific coast of Russia.

The Turkish empire had been decaying since 1822, when her boundaries had included (in modern terms) Yugoslavia, Rumania, Bulgaria, Albania, Greece, Jordan, Egypt and Libya. Turkey, at that time, was ruled by the Sultan, Mahmud II, backed by a chief minister and a council of ministers called the Divan. The whole government was known as the 'Sublime Porte'—that is 'the gate'—the place where, traditionally, magistrates and princes sat to administer justice.

In Mahmud's reign, rebellion first broke out in Greece. Idealists from all over Europe hastened to join the Greek guerrillas, while Mahmud was forced to call on help from Mehemet Ali, ruler of Egypt, to suppress the rising. It was here that Lord Byron died of fever in 1824—his 'martyrdom' for the Philhellene cause doing much to prod the reluctant governments of Britain and France into action, fearing that if they did not get into Greece, Russia might 'liberate' that country, and thus acquire an outpost in the Mediterranean. Although the guerrillas were defeated, resistance continued until 1827, when the allies sent a fleet to blockade the Turkish-Egyptian army in the Morea. The allied fleet entered the bay of Navarino during a period of armistice, and anchored alongside the Turkish-Egyptian fleet. A British captain sent a boat over to the Turkish admiral to ask him to remove a fireship anchored dangerously to windward. The Turks opened fire on the British boat and the engagement became general, resulting in the total destruction of the Turkish fleet. The Sultan, refusing to accept the excuse that the engagement was unintentional, proclaimed a holy war against Christendom. In 1828 Russia invaded Turkey, crossing the frontier on the River Pruth and coming down the classic invasion route from the north, through Silistra, Sumla (Sumen) and Varna, over the Balkan passes to Adrianople, at the same time directing an attack through the Caucasus to defeat the Turks at Erivan. The pattern was to be repeated at the start of the Crimean war twenty-five years later.

The Turkish-Egyptian army was thrown out of Greece. After two years of war, the Treaty of Adrianople in 1829 gave independence to Greece, and to the Danubian provinces of Moldavia and Wallachia.

Two years later, Egypt broke away. Her ruler, Mehemet Ali, and his son Ibrahim, who had commanded the repressive army in Greece, thrust northwards through Gaza, Jerusalem, Acre, and Damascus, captured Syria, and crossed the Taurus mountains, defeating the main Turkish army at the Battle of Konya.

Mahmud called on Great Britain for help. In spite of appeals from Sir Stratford Canning, the British representative in Turkey, Lord Palmerston, the British Foreign Secretary, refused to intervene. Mahmud, in a panic, turned to Russia; the Czar, Nicholas I, gladly sent his fleet into the Bosphorus. Mahmud called on Mehemet Ali to withdraw, but the Egyptian ruler demanded Syria, Aleppo, Damascus and Adana as his price. Britain and France, anxious to get the Russian fleet away, put pressure on the Sultan to accept. The Egyptian demands were met, while Russia retained the right by the treaty of Unkiar-Skelessi (1833) to pass ships through the Dardanelles, which could be closed to other powers. In 1839 an attempt by Turkey to recapture Syria was defeated. Mahmud died as the news was coming through, and was succeeded by his son Abd-ul-Mejid I, a boy of 16.

The five powers, Russia, Great Britain, Austria, Prussia, and France continued to work for a settlement of the 'Eastern Question'. France, supporting Egypt, attempted to make a secret settlement with Turkey. The other four powers, in their turn, signed a convention with Turkey in 1840, without consulting the French, who, offended by what they considered a 'deadly affront', prepared to go to war. The British fleet sailed to Beirut; the Syrians rose in revolt against Ibrahim, while Beirut and Acre surrendered to the fleet. The Sultan declared Mehemet Ali to be deposed, but was persuaded by the combined powers to allow him to be named as hereditary Pasha of Egypt.

This brief summary gives some indication of the part played by Britain, France and Russia during the disintegration of the Turkish empire. Austria was also involved; as nearest neighbour to the Danubian provinces she was always sensitive to any Russian movement in this area, and towards the Balkans. In 1848, Franz-Josef I, then a boy of 18, succeeded to the throne on the abdication of his uncle. Franz-Josef had vague dreams of reviving the Holy Roman Empire, but he lacked either the political or military skill to realize his ambitions.

One of the first acts of his government was to issue a proclamation declaring his intention to 'unite all lands and peoples of the monarchy in one great state'. The Hungarian leader Kossuth, challenging the legality of the proclamation, declared the independence of Hungary.

Nicholas I offered help to Franz-Josef and a Russian army invaded Hungary from the north while an Austrian army marched in from the west. The revolution was broken; Kossuth fled to Turkey, while Austria and Hungary reached a compromise over the constitution. As a result of the Czar's aid, Franz-Josef was to remain in a state of vacillating neutrality towards Russia; it will be seen later how much this fact was to contribute towards the failure to avert war in 1853.

Nicholas I soon returned to his plan to expel the Turks from Europe. By the treaty of Bucharest in 1812, Russia's frontier with Turkey had been established on the River Pruth, while Russia had been given a 'right of intervention' on behalf of the Christian subjects in the two Danubian principalities of Wallachia and Moldavia, which lie between the Pruth and the Danube. This right of intervention to protect the members of the Greek Orthodox Church in a Moslem country was one of the main themes of the Eastern Question, and a constant excuse for invasion or war.

In 1850 a quarrel arose over the Holy Places in Jerusalem

—a religious dispute, which hardly seems an adequate cause for war; yet so deeply rooted were the enmities between the governments involved, and between the rulers themselves, and so ready were their people to fight, that in spite of many efforts to prevent war, the great powers were now drifting inexorably towards collision.

The whole matter was aggravated by the character of Napoleon III, the ruler of France and nephew of Napoleon Bonaparte. A political career had brought him to the Presidency of the French Republic in 1848. In 1850 he staged a *coup d'état*, which resulted in his proclamation as Emperor of France in 1852.

He had in his youth been a member of the *Carbonari*—an Italian secret society aimed at the liberation and unification of Italy. He also saw himself as the heir to the Napoleonic legend, casting himself in the role of champion of liberal Europe against the Russian autocrat. He hated Nicholas I, who had insulted him by refusing to address him as an equal, and was determined to enhance his own prestige and that of France at the expense of Russia, and thereby avenge the defeat of 1812.

Kinglake describes the quarrel over the Holy Places as follows:

'Stated in bare terms the question was whether, for the purpose of passing through the building into their grotto, the Latin monks should have the key of the chief door of the Church of Bethlehem, and also one of the keys of each of the two doors of the Sacred Manger, and whether they should be at liberty to place in the sanctuary of the Nativity a silver star adorned with the arms of France.'

These rights had originally been agreed in a treaty of 1740, between the French and the Sultan, confirming the privileges of the Roman Catholic Church in Palestine, but the French had not previously insisted upon their enforcement. Now, however, this attempt by the French to encroach upon the property of the Greek Church, drove the Greek Orthodox priests into a frenzy, and greatly annoyed the Czar. The

French Ambassador, Lavalette, was sent to Constantinople to present the French demands to the Porte. The Porte, unwilling to offend the Greeks, refused the demands. Lavalette threatened to send the French fleet into the Dardanelles and French pressure was gradually increased, until, in December, 1852, the star was actually placed in the sanctuary, and the keys were handed over to the Roman Catholic monks. In the ensuing riots, some Orthodox priests were killed and Turkish police were accused of conniving at their murder.

At the same time, trouble broke out in Montenegro, where a Turkish force under Omar Pasha was operating against the Christians. Austria called on the Sultan to withdraw the Turkish forces; Czar Nicholas backed this demand with an ultimatum to the effect that the refusal of the Sultan to withdraw Omar Pasha's force would be treated as grounds for a declaration of war. The Czar also demanded the restoration of the *status quo* in the Holy Places.

On 2 March, 1853, Prince Menshikov, the Russian ambassador to Turkey, put these demands formally before the Sultan. Only a few weeks before at a reception in St Petersburg, in a conversation with Sir Hamilton Seymour, the British ambassador, Nicholas I had said that he felt it was essential that the two Governments should be on the best of terms, and that Sir Hamilton should convey this message to Lord John Russell. Sir Hamilton had answered by asking the Czar to add 'a few words which might calm the anxiety with respect to the affairs of Turkey'. The Czar replied that Turkey was in a very disorganized condition. 'We have', he said, 'on our hands a sick man—a very sick man; it will be a great misfortune if one of these days he should slip away from us, especially before all necessary arrangements are made.'

A fortnight later the Czar saw Sir Hamilton Seymour again. This time he said that his country was already so large that it would be unreasonable to desire more territory. But he felt that it was his duty to look after the interests of the

Christians in Turkey, a country which had by degrees fallen into a state of decrepitude. He would not tolerate it, however, if England thought of establishing herself in Constantinople. He, for his part, was not disposed to establish himself there, but it could happen that circumstances might force him to occupy Constantinople. 'The sick man is dying—we can never allow such an event to take us by surprise—we must come to some understanding.'

From these conversations, Sir Hamilton Seymour decided that the Czar was proposing to 'carve up' the Turkish Empire. The British Government, however, declined to enter into any secret treaty with the Czar for the settlement of the Eastern Question.

Soon after the arrival of Prince Menshikov with the Czar's demands, a formidable Briton returned to Constantinople as ambassador. This was Lord Stratford de Redcliffe, already mentioned as Sir Stratford Canning, whose whole career as a diplomat had been concerned with the Eastern Question. As *chargé d'affaires* he had negotiated the Treaty of Bucharest in 1812; in 1825, as ambassador, he had tried to find a peaceful settlement to the Greek revolt; later he was to intervene in the Eygptian rising. He was regarded in England as the ultimate authority on affairs in Turkey, where he was accustomed to wield his power and influence without question.

A duel of wits now followed between Lord Stratford, the diplomat, and Prince Menshikov, the general. Menshikov arrived full of bombast and threats; Lord Stratford skilfully isolated the dispute over the Holy Places from other issues, and before long, achieved a settlement. Menshikov continued to press his demands for protection of the Greek Church in Turkey which the Porte, stiffened by Lord Stratford's backing, rejected. The Czar, angered by the approach of the French Mediterranean fleet—a manœuvre carried out without the knowledge of her allies—pressed on insistently; but the Porte firmly refused to grant the Russians the right to 'protect' the Greek Church. Lord Stratford assembled the ambassadors of France, Austria and Prussia, who jointly expressed their desire for a peaceful settlement. But it was too late; on 21 May Menshikov broke off diplomatic relations and left Constantinople.

Ten days later, Count Nesselrode, the Russian Foreign Minister, issued an ultimatum to Turkey, giving her eight days in which to conform, otherwise the Russian army, 'by force, but without war,' would cross the frontier to enforce the Czar's demands. As the eight days went by, the British fleet joined the French in Bashik (Besica) Bay, just outside the Dardanelles. The Porte refused the ultimatum, but, on Lord Stratford's advice, expressed their reply in polite terms, which left open the door to further negotiation.

On 2 July the Russian army crossed the Pruth into Moldavia and Wallachia. Britain and France looked to Austria and Prussia, whose governments declared themselves entirely united in support of Turkey. It seemed that the four western powers were acting in harmony, but this harmony was upset by bad diplomacy. It was Austria which should have led the protest against the invasion of the Danubian Principalities, supported by the powers. But France and Britain, having come to a secret and separate understanding, made it clear that they were to take the lead in action against Russia. Kinglake gives this 'separate understanding' as the point of no return in the efforts to avert war. The Austrian army was on the spot; it was Austria which was most affected by the invasion; the fact that it was France and Britain who took the initiative was a needless provocation.

Having come to a separate understanding with Britain, Napoleon III insisted on using the combined naval power of the two countries against Russia. While the Russian armies advanced to the Danube and through the Caucasus to the borders of Persia, the allied fleets were to be brought up to Constantinople, eventually to enter the Black Sea. Early in September, at the instigation of the French, three frigates from each fleet sailed up the Dardanelles and entered the Bosphorus.

The allies, in conference at Vienna, issued Note after Note, each of which was refused in turn either by Russia or by the Porte. The Sultan had no choice left; his people were calling for war; on 5 October, 1853, Turkey declared war on Russia.

CHAPTER II

War on
the Danube

Although Turkey was at war with Russia, Russia was not yet at war with Turkey. The invasion of the Danube Principalities was not 'as an act of war' but 'as a military occupation to prevent internal disorder'—a pretext which has come to sound familiar nowadays.

Omar Pasha, the Turkish commander on the Danube, was instructed to issue a manifesto to Prince Gorchakov, the Russian commander in the Principalities, to the effect that unless the Russians withdrew within fifteen days the Turks would begin hostilities. The Porte, however, would neither place an embargo upon Russian ships, nor would they close the straits to merchant vessels. Gorchakov replied that Russia was not at war with Turkey, but that he had orders not to leave the Principalities until the Czar received the 'moral satisfaction' that he demanded.

The Sultan then invited the allied fleet to enter the Black Sea; but the allies refused to go further than Constantinople on the grounds that the western powers were not at war with Russia. The Turkish foreign minister pressed the admirals and the ambassador to consider the danger to the Black Sea coast and to the Turkish fleet in Black Sea waters. The admirals, however, had no orders to enter the Black Sea, and none were yet forthcoming.

Omar Pasha's army was based at Sumla, 60 miles inland from Varna, his supply port, his right flank resting on the sea. He did not intend to defend the Dobruja, the marshy tongue of land between the Danube and the sea where the great river

RUSSIA

R. Pruth

Jassy

AUSTRIA-
HUNGARY

RUMANIA

R. Arges

R. Oltu

...sova

Galatz

Braila

Macin

Tulcea

R. Danube

DOBRUJA

Bucharest

Trajan's Wall

Constanta

Oltenitza

SILISTRA

static
defence

Citate

Giurgevo

Turtucaia

Vidin

Kalafat

Ruschuk

Calarash

R. Danube

Rahova

Nikopol

Sumla

Yeni
Bazar

VARNA

BALKAN   MTS

BLACK SEA

Burgas

BULGARIA

ADRIANOPLE

TURKEY

MACEDONIA

CONSTANTINOPLE

SCUTARI

GALLIPOLI

⇨	Russian
⇨	Turkish
⇨	French
⇨	British

0   50   100
                        miles

turns northwards. Instead, his defences ran along the line of Trajan's Wall, a former frontier work of the Roman empire; the wall runs from the Danube to the sea port of Constanta. On the southern bank of the Danube were a number of fortified towns, of which the most important were Macin, Silistra, Turtucaia, Ruschuk (Russe), Nikopol (at the junction of the Oltu), Rahova and Vidin.

Most of these towns had their 'opposites' on the north bank—to Macin, Braila; to Turtucaia, Oltenitza; to Ruschuk, Giurgevo; to Rahova, Kalarash; to Vidin, Kalafat.

Omar Pasha was born Michael Lattas, the Greek Orthodox son of a Croatian soldier in the Austrian army. He entered the army at an early age, but was forced to leave his regiment when scandal overtook his father. Michael left the country, and wandered homeless for a time, until he found employment as tutor to the sons of a Turkish businessman. To get the job he had to become a Mohammedan; at the same time he took the name of Omar. He next graduated to the post of instructor in a military college, and later became ADC to a Turkish general, under whose patronage he made his way into Turkish society. He married a rich heiress, and was appointed military governor of Constantinople. In 1848 he was put in charge of the Turkish forces in Moldavia and Wallachia during the suppression of Kossuth's rebellion. His handling of this difficult mission alongside the Austrian and Russian armies had showed him to have diplomatic as well as military ability. He then commanded operations against Bosnia in 1851, and Montenegro in 1852. Now, in 1853, he was supreme commander of the Turkish army.

Omar was ordered to break down all the bridges and to remain on the defensive. But he was too good a general to obey this policy; he intended to retain the ability to cross the Danube and to harass the enemy on the farther side. His general strategy was to keep his left flank strong and mobile as a threat to the Russians, should they push back his centre; at his back were the Balkan passes, strongly defended natural fortifications. His first thought, however, was to take the offensive, to 'blood' his troops, and to raise their morale by an early victory.

The Turkish army was one of the oldest standing armies in Europe. The soldiers had formerly been the 'yani-tcheri' (literally new troops) or Janissaries, members of an élite corps largely recruited from Albania, Bosnia and Bulgaria. But like all élite corps, in every army, they were apt to become 'too big for their boots'. They were often conspicuously lacking in their respect for the Sultan and their favourite method of protest was to set fire to Constantinople. Efforts on the part of one Sultan, Selim III, to replace them in 1806 by a new and more disciplined force, led to his dethronement, followed by a pitched battle between the Janissaries and their intended replacements. The Janissaries were beaten off by artillery, but the new force had to be disbanded, leaving the Janissaries more truculent than ever.

Sultan Mahmud II determined to be rid of them and raised yet another new corps of regulars known as *eshkenjis*. In June, 1826, the Janissaries rose in revolt and tried to bring out the *eshkenjis* with them. The Government declared war on the Janissaries, who were surrounded by troops and guns in the Et Maidan square in Constantinople. The artillery commander called on them to surrender; they refused and were shot down, their barracks burnt, and the survivors hanged before the grand vizier.

Mahmud II then proceeded with a thorough reorganization of the armed forces. The existing naval and military schools were reformed and foreign instructors were imported. Abd-ul-Mejid continued with this policy; more military schools were opened, and the recruiting law was changed, reducing military service from an indefinite term to a limited period. There were many Englishmen serving with the Turkish forces, where the peculiar aptitude of the English for inspiring the trust of foreign troops was often put to good account.

Omar's opponent, Prince Gorchakov, was a general of some experience who had fought in the Russo-Turkish war of 1828. More recently he had been Chief-of-Staff of the Russian army, and Adjutant-General to the Czar. Now he was appointed as Commander-in-Chief of the forces detailed to invade the Danubian Principalities.

The Russian army was not considered in Europe to be a first-rate weapon for offensive warfare. Czar Nicholas's reign had opened with a mutiny of the army, in a country that his brother had left disorganized and demoralized. Nicholas was only interested in military affairs; he determined to right the disorder by imposing military discipline everywhere, in the civil service, in the universities and in the schools; he also founded the Secret Police as a further agency towards absolute power.

The army was recruited from Poland and from all parts of Russia right out to Kamchatka. In Poland every able-bodied inhabitant between 20 and 30 years old was compelled to serve as a soldier; elsewhere the landed proprietors had to furnish recruits from among their serfs, send them to depots at their own expense, and contribute £12 each towards their equipment. The regular army consisted of the corps of the Imperial Guard, the corps of Grenadiers, and six permanent army corps each of three infantry, one cavalry, and one artillery division. Infantry divisions had two brigades, each of two four-battalion regiments—i.e. eight battalions to a brigade.

Regiments were named after the districts in which they were recruited. In addition to the regular army, there were also the reserve, garrison troops, and irregulars. At the start of the war, the army numbered something over one million men, rising to two million in 1855.

Many of the senior officers were German; two generals, Luders and Schilders, held high appointments at the start of the war; while a young captain of engineers, Franz Edward Ivanovich Todleben, who had served in the Caucasus, and who joined the Danube army, was to have more influence on the course of the war than any other man on either side.

The Russian army which had crossed the Pruth in July, 1853, advanced into Moldavia and Wallachia through Jassy (Iasi) to Bucharest, and occupied the line of the Danube from Orsova in the west, to the Black Sea—a frontage of some 500 miles. Omar Pasha countered by quietly moving a considerable force to Vidin. Then, immediately on the declaration of war, a Turkish force crossed the Danube and entrenched itself at Kalafat, presenting an instant threat to the right flank of the invading army. This move was followed by similar crossings at Braila, Turtucaia and Ruschuk. The Turks fortified their positions on the north bank and awaited the Russian ripostes.

At Kalafat at first there was only skirmishing, since Prince Gorchakov took until January, 1854, to assemble a large enough force for a main assault, which was then defeated at Citate.

At Oltenitza, opposite Turtucaia, about 3,000 Turks held a strong position, covered by artillery sited on a high island in the middle of the river. This island was in turn covered by Turtucaia, which stands 600 feet above the Danube. The Turkish positions were in the angle of the River Arges and the Danube, facing north-east towards the village of Oltenitza. On 2 November the Russians attacked unsuccessfully with 9,000 men: during the night both sides reinforced their troops to about double the strength on the first day; after a similar attack on the second and third days, there was a lull till 11 November, when the Russians tried to capture the island, again without success. Oltenitza was the first Turkish victory of the war—others were soon to follow, at Macin, Kalafat, and Giurgevo, where Prince Gorchakov again failed to cross the Danube.

While Turkey and the allies were rejoicing at the news of these victories, a setback occurred in the Black Sea. A Turkish naval squadron of seven frigates, a steamer, two schooners and three transports, sheltering from bad weather in the port of Sinope, half-way along the north coast of Asia Minor, was surprised by a Russian fleet of three first-raters, three two-deckers, two frigates and four steamers.

Ostensibly, a naval truce still existed, since the Czar, in a circular issued by Count Nesselrode, had declared that he would confine his action to the Danube Principalities, while the Sultan had expressed his ambition to be confined to the expulsion of Russia from that same area.

Admiral Osman Pasha was therefore probably under a false sense of security. The fortifications of Sinope were not in a state of readiness; Admiral Nachimov was favoured by a fog which hid his approach. The whole Turkish squadron was destroyed—'never in naval warfare', writes E. H. Nolan, 'was so horrifying a slaughter before witnessed; five thousand sailors perished, the whole squadron was blown into one mass of broken and burning timber, and blasted and bleeding human flesh. Yet amidst the floating timbers, blackened and blood-stained, the Russian ships fired grape and canister, lest any of the wrecked should swim ashore . . . Oltenitza and Macin were avenged.'

An English steamer escaped, 'considerably damaged', and brought the news to Constantinople. Admiral Dundas suggested that the combined fleets set sail in pursuit at once, but the French ambassador refused to co-operate. It was not until 4 January that the allied fleet entered the Black Sea.

Sinope was regarded as an atrocity by the people of western Europe; it was also felt to be a humiliation, in that the massacre had occurred while the allied fleets were within easy reach. Although it was believed that the action was what we would nowadays call a 'Pearl Harbour', this was not really true; Russia and Turkey were already fighting on the Danube, while at the eastern end of the Black Sea, the Turks had seized the Russian fort of St Nicholas, and were attacking Russia on the Armenian frontier. The Russian admiral, according to Nolan, had broken a naval 'point of honour' not to attack frigates with first-raters, unless first fired upon; but according to Kinglake, the Turks fired first.

Whatever the rights and wrongs at Sinope, the battle

precipitated Britain and France into war. Napoleon III pressed upon the British Cabinet a proposal to give Russia notice that all Russian ships in the Black Sea should return to Sevastopol; and that any act of aggression against Turkey would be met by force. A Note to this effect was sent to the Czar on 12 January, 1854, and five weeks later he broke off diplomatic relations with Britain and France.

During the winter, the Czar removed Gorchakov from command of the Danube army, replacing him by a veteran, Paskevich, who had led the attack on Turkey in 1828. This old, experienced campaigner insisted that the Czar should abandon the idea of holding down the whole of the two Principalities and should concentrate his effort into a single thrust through Silistra, Sumla and the Balkan passes to Adrianople. This plan, he said, would succeed, provided that Silistra could be taken before 1 May. Russian forces were concentrated for this purpose, while the western powers prepared to receive a great invasion of Turkey from the north.

Two engineer officers, Col Ardent from France, and Sir John Burgoyne from England, were sent at once to Turkey to advise the Sultan, while both countries agreed to send a small force of troops to the Mediterranean in readiness to support Turkey. Sir John and Col Ardent produced the unimaginative plan of fortifying the Dardanelles as a base for the allied armies.

Efforts for peace had not been abandoned; Britain, France, Austria and Prussia had issued a Protocol, making the first moves towards a guarantee of support for Turkey; Napoleon III had written personally to the Czar, asking for an armistice to enable negotiations to be reopened; a Quaker deputation had been received by the Czar, who said, however, that he must perform his duty as a sovereign. Austria reinforced her army on the Wallachian frontier. The Czar could have no doubt that all Europe was against him, but he could not believe that the British Government, under Lord Aberdeen, would really go to war.

In this he was wrong; an ultimatum had been issued on 22 February that unless Russia withdrew all her troops from the Principalities by 30 April, Britain and France would declare war.

The British and French Baltic fleets left their home ports early in March, whilst French troops embarked for the Levant. Since no answer was received from the Czar, on 27 March Great Britain and France declared war on Russia.

The Russians were by now already across the Danube. General Luders had crossed at Galatz (Galati) into the Dobruja; Prince Gorchakov, who had been beaten for the second time at Giurgevo, marched to the north-east and crossed at Tulcea; but this combined force was contained according to plan at Trajan's Wall by the Turkish right flank.

At Silistra, General Paskevich himself was in charge of operations. The siege began on 14 April, by the siting of artillery batteries on the north bank of the Danube; in three weeks the Russian forces had surrounded the city.

The fortifications, designed by a Prussian, Col Grach, consisted of a strong semi-circular work of stone, covered by outlying forts on features to the south, east, and west of the town, connected to the main bastions. Guarding the most important of these forts, the Abd-ul-Mejid, was a newly constructed earthwork about 150 yards long, called the Arab Tabia. The Russians could not storm the Abd-ul-Mejid, the key to Silistra, until the Arab Tabia was taken; the Arab Tabia was manned by well-disciplined Egyptians, armed with the French Minié rifle (of which more later), and by Albanians armed with matchlocks. Two young English officers, Capt Butler of the Ceylon Rifles, and Lt Nasmyth of the East India Company's service, had chosen to station themselves in the earthwork, where they took command of the operations. The total garrison of Silistra was estimated at something between 8,000 and 12,000. Concentrated against it was a Russian army of 30,000, which was gradually increased to about 50,000. General Paskevich was advised by Prince Gorchakov, an artillery expert, by General Schilders, his engineer, and by General Luders.

By 28 April, the Russian batteries were in position on the south side, on an island facing the north side, and on high ground to the south-west, facing the Arab Tabia and a second earthwork, the Illanli. Bombardments and assaults followed each other alternately. Omar Pasha remained with his reserves at Sumla, refusing to be drawn into battle; Silistra must fight it out alone. The only relief sent by Omar was a brigade of light infantry under Behrem Pasha—the Turkish name for an Englishman, General Cannon—with instructions to harass the besieging forces from the wooded heights surrounding the town. For week after week, the siege continued; all Europe hung upon the fate of the fortress, while with painful slowness, the Allied armies crept to the aid of the Turks.

The first part of the British contingent had left Malta on 31 March, arriving at the Dardanelles on 5 April, disembarking at Gallipoli, where the French were already encamped. Naturally, the French had taken the best billets, in the Turkish quarter, while the British had to be content with the hostile Greek part of the town. Later contingents, finding no room, were sent on to Scutari, where the whole force was eventually concentrated. Here the British occupied the huge Turkish barracks, later to become famous—or infamous—as a hospital.

Napoleon III ordered Marshal St Arnaud, the French commander-in-chief, to confer with his British colleague, Lord Raglan, and with General Omar Pasha, about the best method of supporting the Turks in Bulgaria—either by marching through the Balkans to Adrianople, or by attacking Odessa, which might then be used as a base for operating against the rear of the Russian army on the Danube. St Arnaud and Lord Raglan went to Sumla to visit Omar Pasha, who urged them to occupy Varna, from which port they could give strong support to his right flank. The allies agreeing, embarkation was begun on 28 May. When the expedition arrived in Varna the siege at Silistra was at its height; the troops could hear the guns, seventy miles away to the north-west.

On 4 June, Marshal St Arnaud suddenly tried to change the plan, by announcing that he would only send one division to Varna, while the rest of the army would remain behind the Balkan range, based upon Burgas. General Bosquet's division was set in motion, to march to Adrianople. Lord Raglan refused to conform to this plan, and insisted on continuing the attempt to join Omar Pasha for the relief of Silistra. St Arnaud gave in; it was not the first time that Lord Raglan had been compelled to apply a firm veto to the plans of his ally. Bosquet's division had, however, gone too far to be recalled, and continued on its weary march to Adrianople.

Meanwhile, the Russians made one attack after another, in their desperate efforts to capture Silistra. They were already six weeks behind the schedule proposed by General Paskevich, who resigned on 8 June, handing command of the army back to Gorchakov.

Omar Pasha's small relieving force under General Cannon actually succeeded in entering Silistra, at a time when the garrison was almost exhausted. Omar Pasha also ordered diversionary attacks to be made at Giurgevo and Oltenitza. On 10 June Captain Butler was wounded, dying of fever nine days later. On 22 June the Russians attempted a final desperate assault—Prince Gorchakov's order of the day contained the disheartening message that the troops' rations would be stopped if the attack failed! Gorchakov and Schilders were both severely wounded; as day broke on 23 June, the besiegers were seen to be retreating northwards across the river; Silistra was saved.

Ten days later a Turkish force, assisted by General Cannon and seven enterprising young British officers, attacked the Russians at Giurgevo. Prince Gorchakov's army, released from the siege of Silistra, arrived, only to be defeated for the third time in the campaign on the same ground. The Russian forces withdrew northwards through Bucharest, and abandoned the Danubian Principalities. The war seemed to be virtually at an end.

CHAPTER III

War in
Asia Minor

While the war on the Danube was holding the attention
of the western world, another campaign was being fought in
Asia Minor. Russia, in her drive to the south, had always had
designs on the eastern provinces of Turkey and on Persia.
After the Russo-Turkish war of 1828, Turkey had been forced
to give up the whole east coast of the Black Sea, from Anapa,
near the entrance to the Sea of Azov, to Poti, just north of
Batum. Russia had put much pressure on Persia to force her to
join in the war against Turkey in 1853. Persia responded with
a few frontier aggressions sufficient to cause a break in diplomatic relations. But when British subjects in Persia were
insulted and attacked, the British *chargé d'affaires*, failing to
get satisfaction owing to the influence of the Russian envoy
at the Persian court, broke off relations with the Shah, and
hinted that Britain would attack from Aden and Afghanistan.
The Persians immediately climbed down and gave assurances
that they would maintain a strict neutrality.

When war between Russia and Turkey was imminent,
the Sultan found a useful ally in Shamyl, a Daghestan chieftain
who had for a long time been fighting the Russians for the
independence of the hill tribes of the Caucasus. Shamyl, a
Mohammedan, had fermented a holy war against the Russian
army of occupation. The Caucasus became for years a theatre
of fierce guerrilla fighting; bands of armed tribesmen
descended from the mountains to attack the chain of forts built
by the Russians to protect their communications in the coastal
plains on the Black Sea and Caspian coasts. It was 'North-West

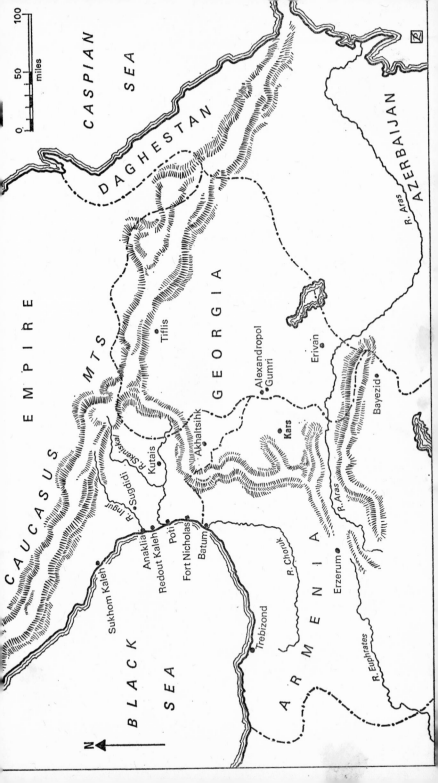

CASPIAN SEA

DAGHESTAN

EMPIRE

CAUCASUS MTS

AZERBAIJAN

R. Aras

GEORGIA

Tiflis

Alexandropol
Gumri

Erivan

Bayezid

Kutais

R. Skenitskal

R. Sugdidi

R. Ingur

Akhaltsikh

Kars

R. Aras

Sukhom Kaleh

Anaklia

Redout Kaleh

Poti

Fort Nicholas

Batum

ARMENIA

Erzerum

R. Choruk

R. Euphrates

Trebizond

BLACK SEA

N

100

50

0

miles

Frontier' warfare, in which the Russian soldier, not schooled in independence or initiative, was at a disadvantage.

Shamyl was a legend; he was believed at one time to have returned from the dead, after being shot and bayoneted in the defence of his stronghold at Akhoulga. A few weeks later he appeared again at the head of a new army. The Russians took the son of another tribal chief to St Petersburg, trained him in the army and sent him back to the Caucasus as a Major-General, to advise the Russian commanders in the field. He immediately deserted to Shamyl, married his sister, and became his right-hand man. This was Daniel Bey, who was to train the tribesmen in European warfare, helped by Polish and Russian deserters.

These then were the formidable allies who were to join the Sultan in 1853. Nolan comments, 'Had the Turkish generals done their part as efficiently and gallantly as Shamyl did his, the Russian Army of Asia had been annihilated before the close of 1853; but never in the history of services were cowardice, folly and peculation so conspicuous as with the Turkish commanders upon that theatre of war.'

When the Russians advanced into the Danubian provinces in July, 1853, a motley force of Turkish irregulars and militia was sent to the Persian frontier, while Batum was strengthened by a contingent of 100,000 men from Omar Pasha's army; among these were many European officers, the most outstanding being General Guyon, an Irishman.

The Caucasian guerrillas 'opened the ball' by attacks on Russian posts on the Black Sea coast. The Russians replied by strengthening the important garrison at Redout Kaleh (between Poti and Anaklia), and by reinforcing Tiflis.

As on the Danubian frontier, the Turks did not wait for the declaration of war, but started making raids across the frontier between Armenia and Georgia. The Turkish General, Selim Pasha, made threatening moves at Bayezid in early August, in front of the Russian General Bebatov, and was immediately defeated by that very experienced commander. Bebatov, taking the offensive, advanced on Kars. Selim and his generals panicked, refused to accept advice from General Guyon, and ran for their lives. Only the artillery commander, Tahir Pasha, stood firm and controlled his guns well; but one vital mountain battery, well-sited on the flank of the enemy, was unfortunately out of his control, and in spite of desperate entreaties from an American officer, Major Tevy, refused to fire a shot. Thirty thousand Turks were routed by half that number of Russians; Kars lay open to the enemy. Bebatov, however, was afraid of Shamyl, who was active to the north on his right flank in the direction of Tiflis, so the victory of Bayezid was not exploited and the Turkish forces were given time to recover their morale.

In October, the Turks returned to the attack, drove in some Russian outposts on the line of the River Choruk, advanced to the frontier and, after three attempts, supported by a naval squadron under Admiral Slade, captured the frontier fortress of St Nicholas, between Poti and Batum on the Black Sea. The Russians made repeated efforts to recapture Fort St Nicholas throughout November, but without success.

The Russians were also in difficulties at Tiflis, where Shamyl had made several successful raids against Prince Woronzov's forces. The Turks from Kars advanced down the valleys to Alexandropol, with the intention of uniting with the Batum army, while the eastern wing under Mehemet Pasha, after forcing General Bebatov to evacuate and destroy the fort at Bayezid, advanced on Erivan. However, the Turks were outmanœuvred; defeats followed rapidly at Akhaltsihk, and at Ongusli, before Kars; at the end of November both sides went into winter quarters, stabilizing the front line until the spring.

It was at the end of November, 1853, that the naval disaster at Sinope occurred, as a result of which the allied fleets entered the Black Sea, though the western powers were not yet at war with Russia. There was, therefore, little naval activity in the winter months, until the declaration of war by Britain and France on 28 March. The British steam frigate

Furious sailed to Odessa to take off the consul and some British subjects who wished to leave. The *Furious* sent in a boat, flying a flag of truce, and both were fired on by the battery on the mole. This act was regarded as a barbarous breach of international etiquette and the admirals resolved to attack Odessa. On 22 April, the combined fleet arrived off the port; twelve steamers, six from each nation, accompanied by rocket-boats, came within range of the port. The warships steamed in 'an ever-repeated circle' in file, firing each time they approached the enemy. The little rocket-boats, firing 24-pounder rockets, stood further in to deliver their missiles. The magazine on the mole was destroyed, several ships were sunk, and great damage was done to the dockyards and to the town. The fleet left Odessa on a reconnaissance to Sevastopol; there a British frigate captured a Russian schooner (by the somewhat dubious ruse of flying an Austrian flag) before being chased away by two frigates and a steamer. The main Russian fleet could not, however, be tempted out of Sevastopol.

The Russian strength in the Black Sea at this period consisted of sixteen ships of the line (of 84 guns or more), seven frigates (of 44 to 60 guns), five corvettes (20 guns), twelve brigs, nine schooners, eight cutters, two yachts, one bombard, and thirty steamers, ranging from the *Vladimir* of 400 horse-power to the *Argonaut* of 40 horse-power. There were also twenty-eight Danube gun-boats, and thirty transports, averaging 300 tons each.

Details of the British fleet are hard to find; Admiralty records are scanty until after the war. The following ships took part in the Crimean campaign at one time or another: twelve battleships, twenty frigates, thirty sloops and gun-boats, six troopships, four storeships, fourteen tenders, six mortar vessels, and two floating batteries. The transport fleet of merchant ships totalled about 150. It would be safe to say that not more than half the number of Royal Navy ships were on station at any one time.

The French fleet consisted of a Black Sea squadron under

Admiral Hamelin, of nine ships of the line (80 guns or more) seven frigates, and nine brigs and small steamers. A second squadron, under Admiral Brouat, including six ships of the line, two frigates, and two corvettes, was stationed in the Greek Islands.

Naval skirmishing continued throughout the summer. The mouths of the Danube were blockaded; another attempt was made to draw the Russian fleet out of Sevastopol; the British steamer *Tiger* (16 guns) ran ashore near Odessa, and was destroyed by a small Russian land force of all arms. The crew were taken to Odessa, where, according to Nolan, the officers 'were made "the lions" of every party, and were received into all the good society of the place . . . the poor people treated the tars well, who, having money to spend found no great difficulty in making themselves favourites with the Russian soldiers, who had none.' The midshipmen were accommodated in the Imperial Naval College, where they were well looked after. Prisoners were, however, generally exchanged fairly often, and *Tiger*'s crew were soon back at duty elsewhere.

By the end of the summer, the naval blockade of all Russian ports was complete. Most of the Russian fleet was locked up in Sevastopol; only the steamer *Vladimir*, cruising adventurously, harassed allied and Turkish shipping, playing the part of the armed raider, capturing her prizes under the noses of the admirals in the western waters of the Black Sea.

The summer campaign in Asia opened auspiciously with the capture of Sukhom Kaleh and Redout Kaleh by British and Turkish naval squadrons, commanded by Sir Edmund Lyons and Hassan Pasha. These forts, and many others along the east coast of the Black Sea, were seized and either destroyed or handed over to Shamyl and his Bashi-bazouks. Inland, however, the army of Asia was in confusion; cholera had struck the troops in their winter encampments; the idle and corrupt pashas had spent the winter 'luxuriating in the fumes of tobacco smoke, the dreams of opium eating, and the languid pastime of the harem'. General Guyon's attempts to reorganize the Turks and to galvanize them into action were absorbed and nullified by idleness and obstruction. On 29 July, Selim Pasha with 10,000 men was again routed near Bayezid; Selim—it was rumoured that he had been bribed by the Russians—turned and ran in the middle of the battle. When news of his cowardice reached Constantinople, he was dismissed from his command by the Porte, and removed from the honorary post of commander of the Imperial Guards. The Russians broke through, captured Bayezid, and advanced to Erzerum. Fortunately a large force of Turks had arrived at Trebizond, released from Varna, following the relief of Silistra; Trebizond was therefore secure. On 7 August, the garrison troops at Kars were cleverly drawn out of their fortifications, on to a well-dug Russian position, where they were cut to pieces by the cavalry.

Reinforcements from Trebizond and Batum were rushed to Erzerum and Kars, while Shamyl saved the day again by appearing out of the mountains of Daghestan at the head of 20,000 men, heading for Tiflis. The Russians at Kars and Alexandropol hastily burnt what they could not transport, and withdrew to the rescue of Tiflis. The tables were turned; Guyon tried to persuade the pashas to exploit this sudden change in their fortunes; they replied by petitioning the Porte for his removal. His place was taken by Col Williams, who was untiring in his efforts to expose the corruption of the pashas.

As a second winter came on, Shamyl withdrew once more to his mountains and the Turks were left in possession of Kars and Erzerum. A handful of European officers tried to keep up the morale of a disintegrating army under the most wretched conditions, aggravated by cold, lack of clothing and supplies, while the pashas returned to the pleasures of tobacco, opium and the harem.

CHAPTER IV

War in
the Baltic

On 5 July, 1853, when the news of the Russian invasion of the Danubian Principalities reached London, Admiral Sir Charles Napier went to his desk to write a letter to the Prime Minister. He pointed out that war with Russia was now certain, and that she had in the Gulf of Finland twenty-seven ships of the line, and many smaller vessels, with which she might, in the event of war, threaten the English coast, where there was practically nothing to oppose her. The British fleet was in the Mediterranean, leaving only guard-ships and blockships in home waters. Moreover, the complement of these ships was between three and four thousand men below strength.

Sir Charles recommended that the Home Fleet should be brought to a state of 'discipline and completeness', not only as a matter of justice to the Admiral who was to command it, but also as a matter of first importance to the safety of the country.

Lord Aberdeen replied that he would wait and see what happened. Sir Charles continued to bombard other Cabinet ministers, by letter and interview, but with little effect. However, by November, alarming preparations by the Russians in the Baltic were reported by the Foreign Office. Sir James Graham, First Lord of the Admiralty, unexpectedly wrote to Sir Charles, saying that he would not, as intended, appoint him to the North American station, but would keep him ready to hoist his flag 'nearer home'. Sir Charles was surprised, since he had not sought the American

THE BALTIC

Tornea
Uleaborg
Brahestad

NORWAY
SWEDEN
GULF OF BOTHNIA
FINLAND

Lake Ladoga
Svastholm Viborg
& Bay of
Lovisa
Nystad Helsingfors Kronstadt
Abö Fredriksham
ALAND Hango Sveaborg St.PETERSBURG
Is. GULF OF FINLAND
Bomarsund
STOCKHOLM Revel
ESTHONIA

BALTIC SEA

Gotland
LIVONIA
Riga
KURLAND
Memel
RUSSIAN

DENMARK
COPENHAGEN
Köge Bay
Flensburg
R.Eider Tonning
EMPIRE

PRUSSIA
POLAND

0   50   100   200
└──┴──┴──────┴┘miles

command, nor would he have taken it. He therefore replied
to Sir James that, in the event of war, it seemed that he
would be sent to the Baltic, and in the event of peace to
Sheerness; he was ready and willing for the former, but not
for the latter.

The appointment was made in February, 1854; a fleet
was hastily assembled from ships at Lisbon and in the home
ports, totalling six screw-ships of the line, six steam frigates,
and various blockships and guardships. The chief difficulty lay
in manning these vessels. The press-gang had been super-
seded by a system of bounty offered to each seaman joining

on proclamation of war. War, however, not yet being declared, Sir James declined to issue the necessary proclamation, and therefore no bounty was forthcoming; only a handful of men came forward. The Baltic ice would soon break up; it was feared that a Russian fleet might slip out and begin operations against the British coasts and commerce.

The Board, anxious to get a Baltic squadron away to sea, accepted men well below the required standard for the fleet; mates and midshipmen could not be found. In the end the Baltic squadron was forced to sail on 11 March undermanned by untrained crews.

The squadron consisted of four screw-ships of the line, four blockships, four frigates and three paddle steamers; other ships were to join later. With this little force Sir Charles Napier was ordered, first, to prevent any Russian ship from passing from the Baltic into the North Sea; secondly, to protect Danish and Swedish vessels and territory from attack by Russia. The British Government was anxious to prevent any inclination on the part of these two countries to co-operate with Russia.

The squadron sailed first to Kiel, and thence to Köge Bay, south of Copenhagen, from where Sir Charles felt that he could best dominate the exits to the North Sea.

The British fleet was to be supplied from Flensburg, a good port at the south-eastern corner of Denmark, where an enterprising British businessman, Mr Peto, had obtained a concession from the King of Denmark to build a railway across to Tonning (Tondem) on the River Eider. This railway, together with his fleet of steamers, Mr Peto placed at the disposal of the British government.

The sea-route from the Baltic to Russia lies through the Gulf of Finland, a two-hundred-mile channel, leading to St Petersburg (Leningrad), then the capital of Russia. The defences to the Gulf of Finland were based on four main strong-points; first, Kronstadt, a heavily-fortified island blocking the final approaches to St Petersburg; secondly, the fortress of Sveaborg guarding the entrance to Helsingfors

(Helsinki); thirdly, Revel (Tallinn) on the Esthonian coast, and lastly, Bomarsund, in the Aland Islands. There were also other lesser forts at Abö (Turku) and Hangö in Finland. Ice closed the Gulf completely from December until April.

The Russians had twenty-seven sail of the line in the Gulf, with ten frigates, seven brigs, nine steamers, and many small gun-boats. The main fleet was divided almost equally between Kronstadt and Sveaborg. In all approaches to the ports, the Russians were reported to be laying mines and 'infernal machines'—mines which could be detonated by electricity. The Russians were also said to have allotted 30,000 troops for the defence of the Gulf.

When Sir Charles Napier arrived at Copenhagen he heard that the Russians were hoping to take advantage of the early spring, to unite the Sveaborg and Kronstadt squadrons, still icebound in their harbours. When this information reached London, Sir James Graham sent orders to Sir Charles Napier, that when he was sure that the whole of the enemy's force was in front of him, i.e. in the Gulf of Finland—he should try to keep them shut up there, and then look to the Aland Islands, where a success would have a great effect on both Sweden and Finland.

At Copenhagen, the fleet was exercised in sail-training and in gunnery—the latter, as always, hampered by instructions from the Admiralty to 'hold hard on the expenditure of shells for practice'.

On the declaration of war on 28 March, Sir Charles was ordered not only to blockade the Gulf of Finland, and such other Russian ports as he could cover, but also to cut off all supplies from Finland to Aland, and to report on the possibility of offensive action against Bomarsund, Revel, and other fortified places in rear of his line of blockade.

Reconnaissances were sent to Bomarsund, and to Sveaborg, which was reported free of ice. Sir Charles followed with the main fleet from Copenhagen on 12 April, arriving at the entrance to the Gulf of Finland five days later. Here he found fogs and gales and all lighthouses extinguished.

Without local pilots, and with his inefficient crews, he could not stay in such dangerous waters, but withdrew the fleet to Stockholm to await better weather. There he visited the King, in the hope of persuading him to throw in his army on the side of the allies. His Majesty listened patiently, but would not shift from his position of neutrality.

In May the weather improved and the fleet sailed to Hangö, where a few shots were exchanged with the garrison. In June the fortifications of Sveaborg were examined, and found to be too strong for any guns mounted in the ships of the fleet. One squadron, under Admiral Plumridge, was sent north to Aland and the Gulf of Bothnia, where much damage was done to Russian merchant ships and naval stores at Brahestad (Raahe) and Uleaborg (Oulu). At Tornea, however, the expedition nearly met disaster; the landing party ran into a strong force of Russian regular troops, and only escaped with considerable losses.

On 21 June, Capt Hall, who had been left by Admiral Plumridge with three ships to watch Bomarsund, took advantage of the presence of a local pilot to attack Bomarsund on his own initiative. He anchored out of range of the guns in the forts, and bombarded them for eight hours, claiming to have done much damage. Having spent all his ammunition he withdrew. In fact, apart from setting fire to a few outbuildings, it is doubtful whether anything was achieved except an extravagant waste of powder and shot.

On 22 June the allied fleet, now numbering twelve British and six French sail of the line, with nine steamers, set sail for Kronstadt, leaving nine sail of the line and six frigates to watch Sveaborg. On 26 June, the fleet arrived off Kronstadt, beyond which the Russian fleet of thirty sail was anchored in three columns. Three days were spent in careful reconnaissance, revealing the fact that the fortress, which bristled with guns, could not be approached except by ships of shallow draught, and that to attempt an attack with no special artillery, mortars or rockets, with eighteen capital ships against twenty-two of the enemy, would be an act of madness, playing into the Russians' hands. Nevertheless Sir Charles Napier was severely criticized later for not attacking Kronstadt with the fleet alone—a fleet in which cholera had recently broken out.

The allies therefore withdrew from Kronstadt to Sveaborg, where Admiral Corry, with the squadron on watch, had made a careful examination of the defences. Sveaborg was defended by booms, stakes, mines, and 8,000 troops in very strong granite fortifications.

On 2 July Sir James Graham wrote to say that 6,000 French troops, with ten guns, were to be sent in British ships for the Admiral to use either against Sveaborg or Bomarsund —preferably the latter. The Admiral replied that Bomarsund would be the most profitable objective.

Bomarsund guards the northern and most practicable entrance to the great landlocked harbour of Aland; the town stands on a spit covering the narrow channel between the mainland and Prästo Island to the east. The shore-line of the spit was guarded by a semi-circular fort at water-level, holding 120 guns in two tiers. On the landward side, the granite forts Tzee and Nottich crowned the tops of twin hills, guarding the approach from the flat ground behind the town. These red granite towers, with their bomb-proof iron roofs, contained twenty-four guns each; other defences, however, were incomplete on the landward side.

The army available for the attack consisted of about 10,000 French troops commanded by General D'Hilliers, and 1,000 British, under Brigadier Jones of the Royal Engineers. The expedition embarked at Calais in British ships, arriving off Aland early in August.

The landing was made four miles north of Bomarsund on 8 August, the advanced guard being a contingent of British marines and sappers, followed by a brigade of French marines. The main body of the French landed south of Bomarsund at the same time. The forts were invested; batteries were placed in position to attack the round towers. By 13 August, all guns being in position, the bombardment was begun; the French against Fort Tzee to the west, the British on Fort Nottich to the east. Both forts were silenced, then crumbled to ruins. The French stormed Fort Tzee on 14 August, the British took Fort Nottich on the following day; the fleet bombarded the main fort and Prästo Island; Bomarsund was surrendered unconditionally soon after, and its fortifications were dismantled. Aland was offered to Sweden, but the offer was refused.

The Admiral now turned his attention to Abö in Finland. A reconnaissance showed the presence of seventeen gun-boats, and a large force of riflemen in the thick woods each side of the channel leading to the town. Sir Charles Napier proposed an attack, but General D'Hilliers refused on the grounds that his troops had cholera. In the circumstances the French were unlikely to attack Revel either, so Sir Charles decided as a last resort to investigate the possibility of capturing Sveaborg. General D'Hilliers and his chief engineer were piloted to Sveaborg in a British survey ship with Brigadier-General Jones. The French were unanimous that there was nothing to be done so late in the year. The Brigadier, however, sent in a report that an attack on the fortress could be made by landing guns on a neighbouring island in order to destroy the principal works in the dockyard.

On 4 September the French started to withdraw back to Cherbourg. Sir Charles Napier was ordered to report on further possibilities for the year; but by the time he received these orders, the French had already left.

The blockade on the Russian coast was kept up until the end of October, when the fleet was gradually withdrawn, first to Kiel and thence to Spithead, where on 22 December, the Admiral was curtly told 'you are hereby required and directed to strike your flag, and come on shore'.

This insulting order was the result of a long series of differences between Sir Charles Napier and the Board of Admiralty, for which there is no space here. But the student will find much entertainment in the exasperating instructions issued from Whitehall, giving the 'man on the spot' a free hand, and then circumscribing his activities by niggling detail and impossible suggestions; by orders to do something. followed by reprimands for having done it; by lack of appreciation of local conditions; and above all, by the impossible tasks allotted to a tiny force of ships in a vast theatre of war.

Sir Charles had not lost a ship; he had confined a superior Russian fleet to the Gulf of Finland during the whole summer; he had tied up 30,000 troops which could have been used elsewhere; he had destroyed many merchant vessels, and blockaded all the trading ports in Esthonia and Finland—though he could not prevent a steady flow of coal and war materials to Russia through the Prussian port of Memel, some of it from opportunist traders in the north of England! Lastly, he had captured Bomarsund in a neat and efficient operation. At the end of all this, he was dismissed from his command, without thanks for his services. He began a correspondence with the Admiralty, requesting that his conduct be investigated by court-martial.

Their Lordships replied by declining to 'submit a controversy raised by an officer under their orders to the decision of a court-martial'. Furthermore, they wrote, 'you have repeatedly thought fit to adopt a tone in your correspondence with their Lordships which is not respectful to their authority.'

The Admiral was more than a match for them; not for nothing had he been MP for Marylebone for four years. He produced the Admiralty letters to himself and took them to pieces mercilessly, paragraph by paragraph, exposing their contradictions and misrepresentations one by one. The Board of Admiralty hoisted the white flag; Sir Charles continued his attack, calling on Lord Aberdeen for an investigation into the whole conduct of the campaign. But the Prime Minister was in the act of resigning. His successor, Lord Palmerston, was unwilling to grant an investigation, but strongly praised Sir Charles. Finally the Admiralty surrendered completely by recommending Sir Charles for the

GCB, the highest class of the Order of the Bath. Sir Charles had the last word; he refused it!

There were two other interesting naval ventures against Russia in 1854. The first was a partial blockade of the White Sea in July by a small squadron of three British ships— *Eurydice*, a steamship of 26 guns, *Brisk*, a screw-corvette of 16 guns, and *Miranda*. The squadron entered the White Sea late in June, after bombarding Kola in northern Lapland. An attack was made on Solovetski Island in the Gulf of Onega. The squadron boarded and examined over 300 merchant vessels, capturing any that could be fairly claimed as prizes.

Secondly, a combined French and British force, operating in the North Pacific, attacked the Russian naval base at Petropaulovsk on the Kamchatka peninsula. A landing by marines and seamen was beaten off, with heavy losses. The whole affair was clouded by the suicide of Admiral Price, the British commander, who shot himself in his cabin just before zero hour—hardly an auspicious start to the operation for which he was responsible.

CHAPTER V

The Allies Prepare

Let us return to 24 June, 1854. The Danube war seemed to be over. Russia, having failed to capture Silistra, was retreating, her fleets blockaded in their harbours in the Baltic and the Black Sea.

There seemed little reason why peace should not follow. But the impetus of a war-machine set in motion cannot so easily be halted. Napoleon III was longing for a military success to adorn his newly-won position as Emperor. In England the people were on the side of war. *The Times* was pressing the Government to strike at Sevastopol and the Russian fleet: 'the taking of Sevastopol and the occupation of the Crimea . . . would repay all the costs of the war and permanently settle in our favour the principal questions in dispute, and . . . those objects were to be accomplished by no other means, because a peace which should leave Russia in possession of the same means of aggression would only enable her to re-commence the war at her pleasure.'

The decision to attack Sevastopol was taken by the Minister of War, the Duke of Newcastle, almost entirely on his own. On 28 June he sent a private letter to Lord Raglan, saying that the Cabinet was unanimously of the opinion that if he and the French were ready, Sevastopol should be besieged. A dispatch would be submitted to the Cabinet, and would follow. Meanwhile Lord Raglan was to turn over the matter in his own mind, and discuss with Marshal St Arnaud 'what it will be safe and advisable to do'.

Having issued this warning order, the Duke then prepared a draft of his proposed instructions to Lord Raglan, and took it to Pembroke Lodge, Richmond, where on a hot summer evening the Cabinet was in session. Although the dispatch contained a momentous decision, committing the allies to a desperate venture, it was received without a single voice raised in query or dissent, for the reason, says Kinglake, that 'all the members of the Cabinet except a small minority were overcome with sleep'.

Napoleon's telegram to Marshal St Arnaud forbade him to cross the Danube, and told him to prepare to embark his army at Varna; the rest of the message was indecipherable. St Arnaud received the decision to invade the Crimea from Lord Raglan.

The British and French armies lay at Varna. The excitement of arrival in a new and beautiful countryside was already tempered by boredom, frustration, and now by the terrifying threat of sudden death from disease, for cholera had broken out.

The British army at Varna consisted of five infantry divisions (each with two brigades of three battalions); a cavalry division, with a heavy and light brigade, each of five regiments; and seven batteries of field artillery. The 'battering train' of siege artillery was not yet disembarked; half was off-shore at Varna, the rest waiting to leave England.

The Commander-in-Chief, Lord Raglan, was now 75, having spent nearly fifty years in the army. He had been ADC and Military Secretary to the Duke of Wellington in the Peninsula, and at Waterloo (where he lost his right arm), and again from 1827 until the Duke's death in 1852, when he was appointed Master-General of the Ordnance. His bravery was unquestioned—he had been first into the breach at Badajoz—but he had never commanded a formation in the field. Yet, from his years of experience with the Duke he had acquired a sound knowledge of tactics, extreme calm under fire, a fair eye for opportunity in the heat of battle, and not least, an excellent talent for diplomacy, learnt during two spells as Secretary to the Embassy in Paris.

The senior officers of the British Army were as follows:

4

GENERAL STAFF	Adjutant-General—Sir James Estcourt, aged 52. Quartermaster-General—Lord de Ros, soon invalided home from Varna, and replaced by Sir Richard Airey, aged 51.
1ST DIVISION	The Duke of Cambridge, aged 34, grandson of George III, 16 years' service, mostly on the staff.
2ND DIVISION	Sir George de Lacy Evans, aged 66, 47 years' service in India, the Peninsula, America, Waterloo and the Carlist War in Spain.
3RD DIVISION	Sir Richard England, aged 61, 46 years' service in Europe and the Cape.
4TH DIVISION	Sir George Cathcart, aged 59, service in the Napoleonic wars and the Cape. He held a 'dormant commission' appointing him to command of the army, in the event of Lord Raglan's death.
5TH (LIGHT) DIVISION	Sir George Brown, aged 66, service in the Peninsula; recently Adjutant-General.
CAVALRY DIVISION	The Earl of Lucan, aged 54, service with the Russian army against Turkey in 1828. Had retired from the army in 1838.
THE LIGHT BRIGADE	The Earl of Cardigan, aged 57, no active service.
THE HEAVY BRIGADE	James Scarlett, aged 55, no active service.
CHIEF ENGINEER	Sir John Burgoyne, aged 71, service in Egypt, Peninsula, and Waterloo campaign.

Many of the older officers, who had fought against the French, regarded their new allies with hostility and suspicion.

De Lacy Evans was the best of the divisional commanders. The Duke of Cambridge, though keen, had no experience. Sir George Brown was one of the most unpopular officers in the army, being a stickler for correct dress under the most unsuitable circumstances, while Sir Richard England was known as 'The Old Woman'.

Among the infantry brigadiers, however, were many men of experience and skill, who were to lead their troops bravely, and whose fighting ability was to go far to counteract the inefficiency of their generals.

In the cavalry, matters were far worse. The Earl of Cardigan was notoriously inefficient and unpopular, and had many times been involved in unpleasant quarrels and scandals. The Earl of Lucan, his brother-in-law, disliked him intensely. Lucan himself had been a strict regimental soldier, but was now quite out of touch with drill and tactics. Scarlett, a kindly and popular officer, had no war experience.

The French army consisted of four divisions, each of two brigades. There was a detachment of *Spahis* present at the landing in the Crimea, and a further contingent of the *Chasseurs d'Afrique* arrived before the end of September.

Marshal St Arnaud, the French Commander-in-Chief, was 53 years old, and had seen most of his active service in Algeria. He had been in charge of the military operations of the *coup d'état* which brought Napoleon III to the throne of France in 1851. He had left his post at the head of the War Office to take command of the army in the east; but he was already a dying man before the Crimean expedition was launched—he had cancer of the stomach.

His divisional commanders were as follows:

1st Division   General Canrobert, aged 45, had seen much service in North Africa. ADC to Napoleon III during the *coup* of 1851, he now held a 'dormant commission' appointing him to the command of the army in the event of St Arnaud's death.

2ND DIVISION   General Bosquet, aged 44, an artilleryman with service in North Africa.

3RD DIVISION   Prince Napoleon Joseph Charles Bonaparte, aged 32, nephew of Napoleon I, heir to the throne of his cousin Napoleon III. Little experience of active service, but of a studious and scientific turn of mind.

4TH DIVISION   General Forey, aged 50, considerable service in North Africa.

The French generals were much younger than the British, but at the same time there was some indication that they had been chosen as a reward for their services in the military *coup*, rather than for their ability in the field of battle.

In 1850 the British Infantry was still equipped with smooth-bore muskets, the Rifle Brigade being the only unit with a rifled musket (the Brunswick Rifle, successor to the Baker Rifle). Since 1844, experiments had been made with a new French rifle, the joint design of Captains Delvigne and Minié, after the latter of whom it was named. Its principal feature was a new way of expanding the conical bullet to fit the rifling more closely. This weapon of ·702 calibre, was adopted and the first British model was constructed by the Board of Ordnance in 1851 and subjected to trials.

Delivery of the Minié to the troops was begun in November, 1853; the regiments that sailed east had only a token number of the new weapon. The Minié was extremely successful on active service, having an effective range far beyond the 200 yards of the old smooth-bore musket; it was sighted up to 1,000 yards (the Brunswick Rifle was only sighted to 300 yards). About 8,500 of the 1851 pattern had been issued in 1853; the new Enfield (1853) pattern of ·577 calibre was not issued in the Crimea until 1855, by which time some 34,000 of the old Miniés had been supplied to the army.

The Russians had some rifled muskets, firing a large

conical bullet, but most of their small arms were old-fashioned smooth bores, with rather flimsy woodwork.

The artillery of both the allied and Russian armies was roughly the same, though the Russian and French guns were slightly heavier than their British equivalents. The different types of artillery may be classified under the headings of field artillery; rockets (both capable of movement in battle); position artillery for use in fixed defences; siege artillery (or 'battering train') for the reduction of enemy defences; mortars; and naval artillery, the last being used extensively by both sides in the Crimea.

Nearly all guns were still smooth-bored, firing solid round shot, or round shell, fitted with the newly invented time-fuse, and containing shrapnel. Grape and canister were employed at short range against infantry, and the carcass, an incendiary shell, against wooden buildings.

A primitive form of rifling was just coming into use, the Lancaster system—in which the bore and projectile were oval, the bore making $1\frac{1}{2}$ twists from breech to muzzle, giving a considerable increase in range. The bore soon wore out and the gun became inaccurate. Elongated projectiles were to follow after the war.

Broadly speaking, field artillery ranged to 600–800 yards, position and siege artillery to 1,000–2,000 yards, the Lancaster to 2,600, mortars to 2,700. A full list of gun calibres and ranges is given at Appendix VIII.

The Russian artillerymen had an obsession about the disgrace of losing a gun, which often caused them to withdraw from a position when it would have been better to leave the guns behind, or to stay and fight it out. Guns which were captured from the enemy could seldom be removed quickly; it was usual to put them out of action by spiking the touch-hole; but unless this was done by crews specially trained and equipped the spike could be easily removed and the gun got back into action.

The Duke of Newcastle's dispatch to Lord Raglan pointed out that the war on the Danube was over, stressed that no further moves should be made in that quarter, and ordered that His Lordship should 'concert measures for the siege of Sevastopol' unless His Lordship was 'decidedly of opinion that it could not be undertaken with a reasonable prospect of success'.

Lord Raglan was given a free hand to decide where, how, and when, the operation should be conducted. When the dispatch arrived, he showed it to Sir George Brown and asked for an opinion. Sir George asked for information about the Crimea, of which very little was forthcoming, and then said that the 'Great Duke' would have declined the responsibility of such a venture, on such slender information about the enemy; but that Lord Raglan might as well agree to it as the Government were clearly set on it, and if Lord Raglan refused, they would simply send someone else out to command in his place. Lord Raglan replied therefore to the Duke of Newcastle that the invasion would be carried out, but that information about the enemy was lacking, and that there was little chance of obtaining any more.

Conferences were at once called, and planning was begun. The sailing date was fixed for 2 September and embarkation was begun on 24 August. The cholera was still raging, especially among three French divisions which had been marched into the Dobruja as a diversionary move to conceal the preparations for the attack on the Crimea. The British cavalry was in poor shape, having been moved inland to a bare plateau at Yeni Bazar, from where Lord Cardigan had conducted a useless and expensive reconnaissance to the Danube. A fire in the British magazines at Varna had destroyed many valuable stores.

The prospect of a sea voyage, and action elsewhere, had raised the morale of the army, but the cholera had then attacked the fleet, forcing the Admirals to put to sea, in the hopes of driving away the disease. In spite of all these setbacks, the force was embarked by 4 September, but bad weather prevented the fleet from sailing. St Arnaud impatiently put to sea on 5 September, but lost his nerve and returned to join the British contingent which finally left Varna on 7 September. No decision had yet been taken about where the expedition was to land!

Various alternatives had been considered; the British Cabinet had suggested cutting off the Peninsula by commanding the Isthmus of Perekop with the guns of the fleet, not taking into account the fact that the sea on both sides is little more than two or three feet deep. In France the ghost of Napoleon I had been consulted by *planchette*! At a shipboard conference on 8 September, which St Arnaud was too ill to attend, the possibilities of landing at the River Katcha, and at Kaffa (Theodosia), had been considered. Kaffa was, however, too far from Sevastopol and the Katcha was dangerously overlooked by high ground. In the end it was left to Lord Raglan to make a reconnaissance in the yacht *Caradoc*, to decide upon a landing place.

The allies were not only ignorant of the enemy strength, but also of the geography of the Crimea. Nothing was known of the interior, nor of the eastern coast, where a curious feature known as the Tongue of Arabat divides the Sea of Azov from the Putrid Sea, thus providing an alternative land-route to the Isthmus of Perekop. The south of the peninsula is mountainous, the north, flat steppe. To the east, the entrance to the Sea of Azov is guarded by the port of Kertch. In the south-west corner the harbour of Sevastopol, at the mouth of the River Chernaya, lies in a strong natural position, strengthened by fortifications on both seaward and landward sides. The principal town in the interior is Simferopol, on the main road between Sevastopol and the Isthmus of Perekop.

The harbours to the south of Sevastopol are Kamiesh Bay on Cape Chersonese, Balaclava, Yalta and Kaffa. For an invader the first lay too near to Sevastopol, the others were either too small or too vulnerable.

After investigating the southern coast, the party on the *Caradoc* passed near to Sevastopol, where hats were solemnly raised to the watching Russians, then steamed northwards inspecting the mouths of the Rivers Belbek, Katcha, Alma, and Bulganek. Beyond this last river, they came on the long sandy coastline of Calamita Bay, at the north end of which lies the small undefended port of Eupatoria (Kozlov). Lord Raglan made his decision—the landing would take place in Calamita Bay at Old Fort, where the salt lake of Kamishla would protect the left flank of the expedition. After receiving the surrender of Eupatoria, where the Governor insisted on fumigating the 'forms of office' and ordering the allies into quarantine, Lord Raglan ordered the armada to move from its rendezvous off Eupatoria, to anchor off Old Fort. A buoy was to be placed to mark the division between the French and British forces and disembarkation was to begin at dawn on 14 September, the French on the right, the British on the left. At sunrise it was seen that the French had placed the buoy too far to the north. The British were forced to land on a beach separated from their allies by a low bluff. In the event, no harm was done; the landing was unopposed, except by a handful of Cossacks, who nearly captured Sir George Brown, impetuously disembarking with his staff, without a proper escort.

The naval arrangements for the landing were in the capable hands of Admiral Sir Edmund Lyons, second-in-command to Admiral Dundas. Military staff-work was the task of the Quartermaster-General, Sir Richard Airey. Thanks to the willing and skilful sailors, the disembarkation went smoothly. The soldiers landed in full dress, carrying a bag of 4½lb of salt meat, and biscuit of the same weight, great-coat and blanket rolled up in a knapsack, containing also spare boots, socks, shirt and forage cap, a water canteen, part of the mess cooking apparatus, rifle and bayonet, cartouche box and fifty rounds of ammunition for Minié, or sixty rounds for smooth-bore weapons. A diversionary feint landing was made by French troops at the mouth of the Alma.

At Old Fort, the French were first ashore; at 8.30 am they planted a flag and rapidly fanned out across the plain. In the first hour, after 9,000 men had been landed, their outposts were already three or four miles from the beach. The British landing was delayed by the moving of the buoy, but the Light Division was soon ashore, and in position on the bluff separating the two armies. Soon, however, files of sick men were returning to the boats, while others dug graves on the beach for new cholera victims. By the end of the day, the French had three divisions and eighteen guns ashore, the British all their infantry and some of their artillery. The night was made miserable by heavy rain. The British, without tents, were soaked to the skin. The French were protected by little 'dog-tents' which they carried with them. A heavy sea hindered the landing of the British cavalry on the following day and only when this operation was well advanced, was the order given to land tents. The disembarkation of the French 4th division had to be suspended for several hours.

The day of 16 September was spent in reconnaissance inland, mostly by the French, whose cavalry detachments captured a small Russian outpost. St Arnaud hoped to move off on 17 September, but the British were still not ready; 'an immense quantity of impedimenta retarded their operations interminably', says Bazancourt. The advance was deferred until the 18th, and still the British were not ready.

It was not until 19 September that the army began to advance southwards, the French on the right, nearest the sea, their divisions in a diamond formation, within which marched the Turkish contingent (eight battalions) and the artillery. The British, on the left, advanced in a rectangular formation, the divisions each in column. The cavalry formed both advanced and flank guards.

In the early afternoon, contact was made with the enemy on the River Bulganek. The cavalry were keen to charge the opposing Cossacks, but Lord Raglan, on higher ground, could see a large mass of infantry beyond them and therefore withdrew the cavalry. The opposing artilleries fired a few shots, the Russians being driven off by the accuracy of the British nine-pounders. Lord Raglan ordered the whole force into bivouac for the night, in order of battle, expecting a flank attack at dawn.

Next morning, however, it was seen that the enemy had withdrawn to his main position on the Alma. Observers comment on the difference between the French and British after several nights in the open; the British chilled and without method in the preparation of breakfast; the French in good order, warm, dry, and well fed. Both armies now moved off for the first test of the campaign—the attack on the formidable defensive position on the River Alma.

CHAPTER VI

The Alma

On the north side of the River Alma, the direction from which the allies were approaching, the ground slopes gently down to the river. Beyond it, however, the hills leap sharply up to a height of 500 feet, forming a long escarpment. For 4,000 yards from the sea, this slope is crowned by a rocky cliff, pierced only by a few narrow tracks. The river is winding, variable in depth, but fordable in most places. The observer, facing south, who looks down from the allied point of view, would see from right to left, on the near bank of the river, first the village of Almatamac, 1,000 yards from the sea, through which runs a narrow road, just passable for guns and wagons; then, 1,000 yards further east, a large white farm, beyond which a steep path climbs directly to the plateau above. In the centre, the Causeway, the main post-road from Eupatoria, crosses a bridge just on the left, or eastern side of the walled village of Burliuk. After crossing the river, the post-road runs through a wider valley, up to a pass on to the plateau. Behind Burliuk two or three tracks wind up to the heights, on which the Russians had partly constructed a semaphore station, known as the Telegraph. To the left of the post-road, the ground is steep, but no longer precipitous. A high hill thrusts a conspicuous shoulder obliquely towards Burliuk; on the lower slopes of this shoulder, known as the Kourgané Hill, can be seen a large earthwork, with another, somewhat smaller, above and to the left. These are the Great and the Lesser Redoubts, thrown up at Menshikov's orders. They are not true redoubts, being open at the back, but only breastworks, offering no obstacle to troops, but giving some cover to the guns which they hold, twelve heavy guns in the Great Redoubt, nine in the Lesser Redoubt.

Prince Menshikov left the west cliff undefended except for a small detachment in the village of Ulukul Akles. He considered the cliff to be inaccessible to troops, and completely impracticable to artillery. As usual in assumptions of this sort about difficult ground, he was wrong; active troops could climb the west cliff almost anywhere, while the ford and track at Almatamac were perfectly adequate for artillery. The Russian forces were concentrated astride the Causeway. On the Russian left, nearest the sea, there was only a single battalion of the Minsk regiment.

The ground to the west of the Causeway was held by the Tarutin and Brest-Bialystok regiments, with the Moscow regiment in support. No two accounts give the same placings for these regiments, but it seems likely that the Tarutin corps was on the escarpment near the Causeway, with the Brest-Bialystok on its left, in the area of the Telegraph. General Kiriakov commanded this sector.

In the centre, General Gorchakov held the low ground in the Pass with four battalions of light infantry of the Borodino corps and one battalion of Russian riflemen; two of these battalions were thrown forward into the vineyards near the river, while the remainder were kept massed in column. Astride the road, covering the bridge, were two batteries of artillery, known as the 'Causeway batteries'.

On the Russian right, the lower slopes of the Kourgané were defended by four Kazan battalions; the Great Redoubt was covered by four Vladimir battalions; the Lesser Redoubt by four Uglitz battalions; the summit of the hill by four Susdal battalions, supported by two battalions of sailors. In addition to the guns in the redoubts, four batteries of field artillery covered the Pass from behind the shoulder of the Kourgané hill. This sector was commanded by General Kvetinski. The right (landward) flank was covered by a force of 3,000 cavalry—Hussars, Lancers and Cossacks, with three batteries of horse artillery. The whole front was screened by

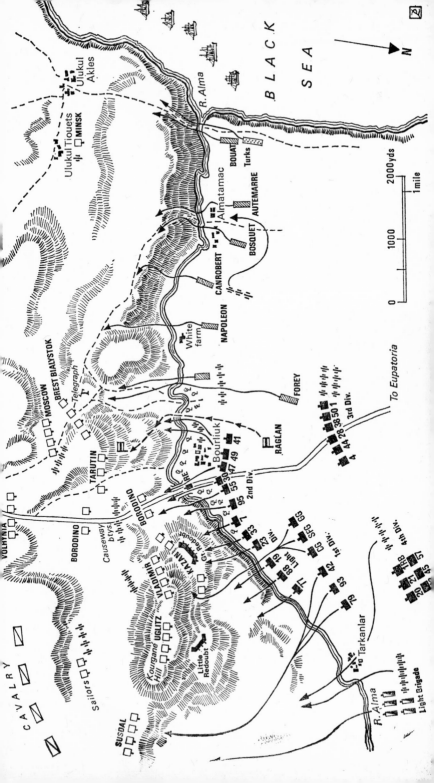

skirmishers ahead of the forward troops, in the cover of the vineyards.

Prince Menshikov's main reserve was on the high ground astride the Causeway road—seven battalions of the Volhynia and Minsk corps, with two batteries of field artillery. On the west side of the Causeway road there were therefore 13,000 men and 36 guns, on the east side 26,000 men with 86 guns. The Prince's headquarters was at first on the Kourgané Hill, but it will be seen later that he spent most of the battle riding desperately from one flank to the other, across a front of over five miles.

The allied plan for the attack on the Alma position was devised late in the evening of 19 September, in the posthouse on the Bulganek, where Lord Raglan had his headquarters. Marshal St Arnaud, attended by Col Trochu, rode over for a consultation with the British commander.

The French had carefully reconnoitred the west cliff from their ships, deciding that the river was fordable right down to its mouth, and that the heights were not strongly held. Marshal St Arnaud proposed that the French and Turks should seize the heights, under covering fire from the fleet, and attack the enemy's left flank, while the British outflanked the enemy's right. He pressed this plan with some force; Lord Raglan kept quiet, and then simply replied that the Marshal could count on the 'vigorous co-operation' of the British army. It was agreed that the French should advance at 5 am followed by the rest of the allies at 7 am.

The advance was begun in silence, without drum or bugle. The French got off well on time, but the British start was delayed, not only by their inefficiency in bivouac, but also by the fact that they had been forced to face east during the night, against the possibility of a dawn attack. To reform and march southwards involved a cumbersome manœuvre, in which there was danger of the reserve ammunition train (in bullock carts) being exposed to attack by enemy cavalry. Lord Raglan, who after years of training with the Duke, was particularly sensitive to any danger to his reserve ammunition, insisted on covering the eastern flank until the slow-moving carts were safely into the new line of march. The result was a considerable delay on the British side and at 9 am orders had to be given to the French to halt. They cooked their coffee and rested until 11.30 am, when both armies were once more level and approaching the River Alma. On the high ground beyond, the troops could see dark squares and patches formed by the enemy battalions drawn up awaiting the attack.

Soon after mid-day, the allied fleet opened fire on the seaward flank. The British forces halted, still out of range of the Russian guns while Lord Raglan and St Arnaud met to decide the part the British should play. St Arnaud asked whether Lord Raglan would turn the position or attack it in front. Lord Raglan replied that in view of the strength of enemy cavalry on the British left flank, he would not attempt to turn the position; it must be attacked in front. The advance was sounded all along the line. As soon as the Rifle battalions, acting as skirmishers, came within rifle range of the Russians in the vineyards on the river banks, the latter opened fire, while the Russian guns on the heights began to try the range. The British therefore halted, and deployed from column into line; the time was 1.30 pm.

On the French front General Bosquet's 2nd Division was nearest the sea. Bouat's brigade was to ford the river at its mouth, while Bosquet himself led the other brigade through Almatamac on to the plateau. On his left General Canrobert's 1st Division was to cross at the White Farm, while Prince Napoleon's 3rd Division was to attack just to the right of Burliuk. General Forey's 4th Division was in reserve. The French were therefore attacking in columns, on a series of narrow fronts; only the 3rd Division came under fire.

The scene on the British side was quite different. Just behind Burliuk, de Lacy Evans with the 2nd Division was deployed in line on a front of about 1,000 yards, while to his left, the Light Division under Sir George Brown was spread out, two deep, over a front of a mile. Behind these two formations, the 1st, under the Duke of Cambridge, was deployed in line on a front of 3,000 yards. Sir Richard England with the 3rd Division was in reserve on the Causeway road, while Cathcart's 4th was drawn up in column on the left flank, behind the left of the leading divisions, and covered by the Cavalry Division under Lord Lucan. Each division was accompanied by its own artillery. Lord Raglan was determined that the operations of the French should take effect before the British army launched its frontal attack; the British were therefore forced to lie under fire on a smooth slope, watching the shot fly through the air towards them. They passed the time in advising their mounted officers which way to move to avoid oncoming cannon-balls, and kept their spirits up by joking among themselves. Any man who was hit was gently lifted by his comrades, who carried him to the rear, and then returned to lie down again.

Ahead of the Light Division, the Riflemen, 'like greenflies', worked their way forward against the Russian skirmishers. As these were forced to withdraw, they set fire, with dramatic effect, to the village of Burliuk, which burst into flames, making it impossible for troops to pass through the streets.

On the French front, things were going well. Bosquet, leading Autemarre's brigade, brushed aside the skirmishers behind Almatamac, forded the river soon after 2 pm, and found the road to the heights unguarded. Soon his leading battalion of Zouaves, with the first of his guns, were on top of the cliff, where they were engaged by four field guns from the village of Ulukul Akles, 1,000 yards away. Bouat's brigade also reached the top unopposed; but they could not get their guns up the cliff and Bouat refused to advance further without his artillery.

General Kiriakov reacted to the sound of gunfire from the west by moving two Tarutin battalions to face Canrobert above the White Farm, and eight guns to cover the approaches to the Telegraph from the seaward side.

Prince Menshikov, on the Kourgané hill, was shocked

to hear that a French division was turning his left flank at the west cliff. At first he refused to believe it; then he rode off hastily, formed up a column of eight battalions from Kiriakov's reserves and his own, and ordered them to march towards the sea. Escorted by Hussars, he rode on to Ulukul Tiouets, where his party came under fire from the ships. His light artillery engaged the French immediately, but his infantry column was still far from the scene. When they did appear, he changed his mind, countermanded his orders, and sent them marching back to the Pass.

Below, in the valley, Canrobert's division was struggling up to the Telegraph Height, without its guns, which had to be sent back to the Almatamac ford. Canrobert also declined to advance from the crest, until they arrived.

Prince Napoleon's division, under fire from the Telegraph area, hung back discouraged, making no progress. The whole situation was becoming precarious. Had Menshikov now acted vigorously against the French on the heights, and with his cavalry against the British left flank, the day might well have been his; but he was galloping wildly from side to side, and gave himself no chance of a calm appraisal of the situation.

Lord Raglan had waited for an hour and a half, with his army lying patiently under heavy fire. He now gave the order for the British infantry to advance. Captain Nolan, Airey's ADC, galloped first to de Lacy Evans, then to Sir George Brown. The whole English line rose from the ground, dressed ranks, and two-deep, two miles long, marched down to the river.

The 2nd Division, cramped between the fires of Burliuk and the right of the Light Division which overlapped it, worked its way through the walls and vineyards near the village, until held up on open ground, swept by the fire of the Causeway batteries.

The men of the Light Division, having crossed the river, found themselves crushed together under the high bank on the far side, being fired on by the skirmishers above them. Their

5

commanders had difficulty in passing on the order to continue the advance up the bank. However, Sir George Brown forced his grey horse up a break in the bank and General Codrington, in command of Brown's first Brigade, scrambled up on his white Arab, while on the extreme right, Col Lacy Yea, commanding the 7th Fusiliers, put his cob at the obstacle and reached the top. The whole brigade surged forward and upwards, towards the Great Redoubt. They were met by two columns of the Kazan regiment, advancing in solid squares towards each end of the brigade. While the troops opposite the Russians engaged them with rifle fire, the centre, led by Codrington, advanced on the Great Redoubt. But before they could reach it, the Russian guns ceased fire, teams of horse were brought down, and soon all but one gun had been removed. The men of the Light Division lay down on the parapet, and prepared to defend what they had won.

The 1st Division, ordered to 'support the Light Division in its forward movement', had at first followed 300 yards behind, but on reaching the vineyards by the river, had come to a halt. The Guards Brigade, on the right of the line, came under heavy fire from both the Great Redoubt and the Causeway batteries. The Duke of Cambridge, in his first engagement, was uncertain what he should do. His doubts were resolved by the arrival of Sir Richard Airey, who on his own initiative ordered the support line forward. After crossing the Alma, the 1st Division came under heavy fire from the Kourgané. An ADC from Codrington came to General Bentinck, to ask for support. Bentinck, commanding the Guards Brigade, ordered the Scots Fusilier Guards forward; but they were not immediately followed by the Grenadiers and Coldstream, who were busy aligning and dressing their ranks as if on parade. At last they began to advance, in an orderly line.

At the Great Redoubt, things were not going well. The Russians were beginning a counter-attack. The four Vladimir battalions, 3,000 strong, advanced slowly on the earthwork, bayonets at the ready. Suddenly the bugle call 'retire' was heard once, then repeated along the British line. The Light Division did not move, until the call was heard again; then the retreat began. Subsequent inquiry failed to discover the origin of this signal, probably attributable to an over-excited staff officer. In the event, the Vladimir battalions took possession of the Redoubt, while the Light Division fell back into the advancing line of the Guards Brigade. For the second time, Prince Menshikov was in a very strong position. The French had made no headway; the centre was held by the Causeway batteries; the British had lost the Redoubt, and were massed in confusion on the lower slopes of the Kourgané. The Russians, however, paralysed by their own ponderous tactics, could not seize their opportunity; there was no 'dash', no *élan*; the Vladimir battalions stood rooted at the Redoubt; the cavalry stayed impassive on the flank. Menshikov himself was still lost; so the troops at the Pass and on the Kourgané received no orders.

Lord Raglan was not in control of the situation at the Kourgané either, though an atmosphere of calm pervaded his staff. ADCs and messengers were forbidden to gallop or hurry, for his Lordship insisted that the watching enemy should never be allowed to feel that the British headquarters was in a state of anxiety or confusion, another legacy from the Duke. Raglan himself was anxious to get a better view of the action than could be afforded by his position behind the 2nd Division. Having ordered the advance, he had ridden down into the valley, close to the blazing ruins of Burliuk, crossed the Alma, and mounted the further slope among the French skirmishers, who were engaged with some Russian 'sharpshooters', whom we should now call 'snipers'. Lord Raglan rode calmly, if somewhat unwisely, through the French, followed by his staff, two of whom were hit by the snipers. A swerve to the left into a gully, followed by a brisk canter uphill, brought him on to a high knoll unoccupied by Russian troops. When he drew rein, he was deep *inside* the Russian position, 800 yards beyond the Alma, above and on the flank of the Causeway batteries. The Tarutin battalions which had formerly held this knoll had been removed to counter the French attack on the west cliff.

Lord Raglan now saw the whole front to the east. Below him were the Causeway batteries; above, in the Pass, stood the Russian reserves, and behind the shoulder of the Kourgané the Uglitz battalions and the sailors waited in support of the Vladimir battalions near the Redoubt. He turned to his staff, 'Our presence here will have the best effect. Now, if only we had a couple of guns!' Col Dickson, of the Artillery, rode off to fulfil the order, while another officer was sent to hasten Adams's brigade from the 2nd Division, which was already on its way.

At this time, Codrington's brigade was just reaching the Great Redoubt. Lord Raglan stood helpless on his knoll, while the Light Division, unsupported by the tardy 1st, was thrown back by the Vladimir battalions.

At this moment a breathless messenger arrived from the French, saying, 'My Lord, we have before us eight battalions.' This threat was from Menshikov's column, collected in his hasty ride to the seaward flank. Raglan promised the French a battalion, which, however, was never required.

The French were still in some confusion. Bouat, Bosquet and Canrobert had not advanced from their footholds on the crest of the cliff. Prince Napoleon had lost a battalion of Zouaves, who had set off on their own to join their countrymen in Canrobert's division. Moreover, d'Aurelle's brigade, from Forey's 4th Division in reserve, having been ordered to join Canrobert on the heights, had marched through the Prince's position and was now jammed nose to tail on the track leading up to the Telegraph. General Kiriakov had fortunately confined his efforts to the heights, for at this moment a determined assault by light infantrymen on the lower slopes could have brought disaster to the French, and might well have captured Lord Raglan and his staff. About this time Prince Menshikov handed over the column of eight battalions to Kiriakov, who led them immediately towards Canrobert; it was this threat which prompted the dispatch of

the messenger to Lord Raglan. Canrobert, however, was
saved by the arrival of his guns, which had been sent back
through Almatamac, to climb the heights behind Bosquet's
division. The French front was therefore secure.

Col Dickson found Maj Turner's battery already crossing the Alma, and two nine-pounders were soon in action on
the knoll, pointing at the flank of the Causeway batteries,
only 400 yards away. It was a gunner's dream. The first shot
missed, the second hit an ammunition wagon behind the guns.
In a few minutes the Russians had limbered up, and galloped
for the Pass. The gunners then turned on to the enemy
reserves in the Pass. After a few minutes the two columns
broke and retreated up the hill. The next target was the
Vladimir battalions, which proved to be out of range. The
Vladimir battalions did not, however, advance far beyond the
Great Redoubt. The Kazan battalions attacking Lacy Yea's
battalion were a better target, and the nine-pounders were
soon cutting furrows through the packed masses of Russian
infantry.

Evans was now free to advance on the Causeway, where
he was joined by Sir Richard England with the reserve
division. Both Generals moved forward together, heading
towards the relief of Lacy Yea's 7th Fusiliers, who were still
holding their ground on the right flank of the Light Division.
The climax of the battle had now arrived; the Guards
Brigade advanced up the slope towards the Vladimir battalions and the Lesser Redoubt, while the Highland Brigade,
further to the left, were mounting towards the eastern slopes
of the Kourgané Hill, held by the Susdal battalions. Both
attacks were soon successful; the Russians abandoned the
position, taking their guns with them.

When the Highland Brigade reached the top of the
Kourgané, the British cavalry could no longer bear to remain
inactive. Without Lord Raglan's authority, they crossed the
river, not without some delay caused by the overturning
of a gun-carriage in the ford, and joined the Highland
Brigade on the uplands. A squadron of the 17th Lancers,

accompanied by Lord Lucan, together with a troop of the 11th
Hussars, set off in pursuit of the enemy stragglers. Unfortunately Lord Raglan was not confident that his cavalry, once
loosed, could be controlled. He therefore ordered Lord Lucan
to call off the pursuit, and to escort the artillery which was
now being brought forward on to the captured position.
This order caused much frustration among the cavalry,
who, restrained at the Bulganek, were again fettered at
the very moment when they thought their chance had come.
Lord Raglan undoubtedly missed a great opportunity, but
he had inherited the Duke's pessimistic view of the British
cavalry, 'galloping at everything, and then galloping
back as fast as they gallop on the enemy. They never
think . . . of manœuvring before an enemy, so little that
one would think they cannot manœuvre, excepting on
Wimbledon Common.' Lord Raglan can have had little confidence in Lord Lucan's ability to manœuvre, since his
Lordship's efforts to drill the Heavy Brigade at Varna had
proved him to be completely out-of-date. It is understandable
therefore that Lord Raglan, commanding an exhausted army,
insecurely perched on a captured position at dusk, far from
its beach-head, was unwilling to let loose his only mobile
reserve into the temptations of a pursuit. Somewhere on his
front or flank 3,000 Russian cavalry, intact and fresh, were
waiting, perhaps to cut him off from his base. He was not to
know that they were even less capable of manœuvre than his
own division. His cautious decision was to fan the flames of
resentment in the cavalry, not least in the mind of Sir Richard
Airey's impetuous young ADC, Capt Nolan of the 15th
Hussars. Had Lord Raglan sent two regiments of the Light
Brigade and a battery of Horse Artillery in pursuit, there
might have been a different story; but he did not.

The Russian army was in complete disorder; only
General Kiriakov faced the front, on a ridge two miles south
of the Telegraph. Here, with thirty guns, and several squadrons of Hussars, he presented a firm rear-guard to the allies.
Lord Raglan saw this position—the Russian cavalry even

advanced a little—in fact he sent a proposal to Marshal St Arnaud that the British cavalry should advance together with one infantry division, and such of the French as the Marshal should think fit. St Arnaud was tired and desperately ill. He replied that further advance was impossible; first because his men had to return for their knapsacks, left behind north of the river; secondly his artillery had shot off all its ammunition.

The battle of the Alma was over, the first battle between European nations for forty years. The French had not emerged with great credit; they could and would do better. The British, amateurish and disorganized in administrative and domestic affairs, had proved themselves against apparently impossible odds.

Their use of the line in attack had been highly successful. They had carried the day against almost equal numbers on ground of the enemy's choice, whereas the French had failed to exploit surprise gained against a numerically inferior enemy. The British generals, old as they were, had led their men bravely, if without much skill; the French, selected mostly for the parts that they had played in the political support of their Emperor, had been found wanting. The Allied *entente* was, however, only slightly damaged and St Arnaud's dispatch was more than generous to the British. The British lost 2,000 killed and wounded, the French 1,300, and the Russians over 5,000. Most writers are sceptical about the French losses, which are believed to be exaggerated by the inclusion of cholera victims.

The Russian army had been fairly beaten on its own ground. Hopes for the campaign now ran high.

CHAPTER VII

The Lost Chances

The troops bivouacked that night on the heights, among the hideous refuse of the battlefield. Next morning the French were ready to move, but now it was Lord Raglan who refused to advance until the dead had been buried and all the wounded had been collected and taken back to the fleet. As the British wounded numbered far more than the French, this operation took all of 21 September, and most of the following day. The French were well equipped with ambulances; the British had none.

Lord Raglan and Marshal St Arnaud now entered into a series of discussions as to the best course to adopt. The original plan was to advance directly across the River Belbek, to attack the North Side, or Severnaya, of Sevastopol harbour. This was defended only by an old fortification known as the Star Fort, sited on high ground behind the sea forts on Cape Constantine, and designed to protect these forts from landward attack. The Star Fort contained 47 guns, distributed all round its circumference, so that only 12 covered the line of approach of an invader from the north. Since the allied landings, the Russians, directed by the engineering genius of Col Todleben, had been strengthening the defences in the area of the Star Fort. Nine additional guns had been sited in earthworks, covering the mouth of the Belbek, but attempts to heighten the parapet of the Fort had resulted in its partial collapse. The whole fortification was vulnerable to fire from the sea, and could also be overlooked from higher ground to the north-east.

On 21 September, Lord Raglan suggested to St Arnaud, at two meetings, that the French should advance to attack the

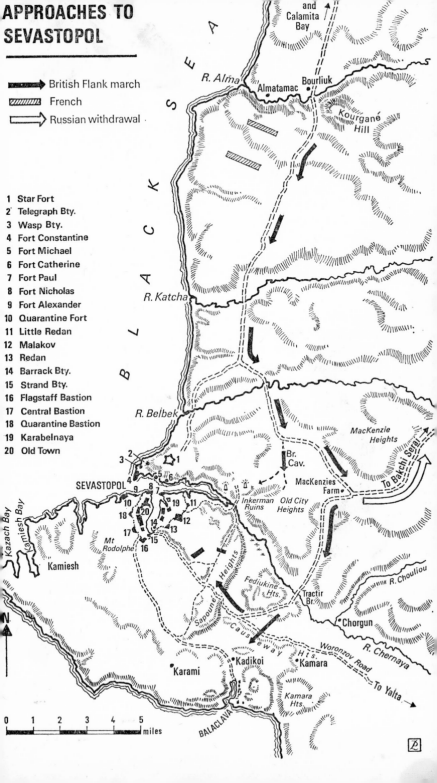

APPROACHES TO SEVASTOPOL

→ British Flank march
/// French
▷ Russian withdrawal

1 Star Fort
2 Telegraph Bty.
3 Wasp Bty.
4 Fort Constantine
5 Fort Michael
6 Fort Catherine
7 Fort Paul
8 Fort Nicholas
9 Fort Alexander
10 Quarantine Fort
11 Little Redan
12 Malakov
13 Redan
14 Barrack Bty.
15 Strand Bty.
16 Flagstaff Bastion
17 Central Bastion
18 Quarantine Bastion
19 Karabelnaya
20 Old Town

and Calamita Bay

B L A C K   S E A

R. Alma
Almatamac   Bourliuk
Kourgané Hill

R. Katcha

R. Belbek

Star Fort (1)
2 3 4 5 6

SEVASTOPOL
9 8 7
10   19   11
18   20
17   14   13   12
15
Mt Rodolphe   16

Kazach Bay
Kamiesh Bay
Kamiesh

Br. Cav.

MacKenzie Heights

MacKenzies Farm

Inkerman Ruins
Old City Heights

To Bakchi Seraï

Sapouné Heights
Fediukine Hts.
Tractir Br.
R. Chouliou

Causeway Hts.
Karami
Kadikoi
Kamara
Chorgun
R. Chernaya
Woronzov Road
To Yalta

Kamara Hts.

BALACLAVA

N

0 1 2 3 4 5 miles

Star Fort, which lay in their sector of the front. St Arnaud refused, first on the grounds that his troops were tired, secondly, that the Russians had thrown up new earthworks covering the Belbek. Nevertheless, on 23 September St Arnaud wrote in a letter to his brother, 'the English are not ready and I am kept back . . . what slowness in our movements!' The fault seems to have lain on both sides.

The advance began again on 23 September, the armies reaching the River Katcha by nightfall. News now reached the allies that the Russian fleet had been sunk across the entrance to Sevastopol harbour. Raglan and St Arnaud held another conference, at which no decision was reached, other than to advance to the Belbek. On 24 September, Lord Cardigan, with the Light Brigade, reported the crossing of the Belbek to be held by a strong force of infantry and cavalry, with some heavy guns, covering a causeway across a marsh. During this advance St Arnaud was taken ill and could no longer sit on his horse; at the evening conference he was in such straits that Lord Raglan could see that he was already dying. The Marshal still refused to agree to an attack on the Star Fort, although information from Sir Edmund Lyons, who had made a reconnaissance from the sea, indicated that the defences were not strongly manned. Lord Raglan therefore put forward another suggestion, which had been forcibly proposed by Sir John Burgoyne, his Chief Engineer.

This plan was to march round Sevastopol to the east, in order to attack from the south, where the defences were weakest. This manœuvre would give the allies the advantage of good bases, in the harbours of Balaclava and Kamiesh, the armies on the North Side now being some thirty miles from their beach-head at Calamita Bay, and ten more from Eupatoria, the nearest port.

As the French would not attack the Star Fort and as Lord Raglan did not feel that he could insult the French by attempting a task in their sector, it was therefore decided that, unless reconnaissance on the following day should produce any further reason to change the plan, the 'Flank

March', as it came to be called, would be adopted. The next morning, St Arnaud was too ill to take any further part in planning. There was therefore no alternative but to carry on with the Flank March on 25 September.

On the 'other side of the hill', the Russian army, after the defeat on the Alma, had withdrawn in confusion into Sevastopol. Admiral Kornilov, in command of the Russian fleet, proposed to put to sea in order to attack the allied armada. He was, however, overruled by Prince Menshikov, who ordered him to blockade the harbour by sinking his ships. When Kornilov refused, the Prince told him to return to his post at Nikolayev, handing over the fleet to his second-in-command. Kornilov changed his mind; the fleet was scuttled, the crews formed into battalions, guns brought ashore and stores and ammunition transported to the South Side.

Menshikov then made an important decision; he would not remain in static defence of Sevastopol, but would remove the army to the north-east, towards Bakchi Serai and Simferopol. He would thus not only keep open his communications with Russia, but would be in touch with any reinforcements coming from Odessa or Kertch; moreover he would threaten the landward flank of the allied armies. On 23 September, General Kiriakov with a flank-guard was sent to the Belbek, where his force was seen by Lord Cardigan on the 24th. On that day the main Russian army marched out of Sevastopol, heading north-east out of the valley of the Chernaya, over the Mackenzie Heights. These were named after a former Scottish settler in the Crimea, whose farm lay on the main road to the interior. The whole area was covered by dense scrub; neither army was aware that the enemy was on the march over the same ground.

Lord Raglan was rashly leading the advance of the British army, having got himself into this exposed position when Lord Lucan took a wrong turning with the advanced guard. Emerging from the scrub at Mackenzie's Farm, he suddenly found the tail of Menshikov's column only a few yards away. He was able to ride quietly back without attracting attention. In a few minutes Lord Lucan reappeared at the head of the cavalry and a short brush followed, in which some wagons were captured.

By nightfall on 25 September the British army was spread out from the Chernaya to the Belbek, the infantry having struggled all day to find their way by compass through the dense scrub, since the only track was occupied by guns and wagons.

On 26 September the British reached Balaclava, which was said to be undefended. Lord Raglan, once more leading the advance without an escort, was fired on by mortars from an old Genoese fort on the heights to the east of the harbour. The officer in charge of the fort surrendered immediately to the Rifle Brigade; the fleet arrived at the same time and thus the British came into possession of Balaclava.

When the French arrived next day, they claimed a share in the facilities of the harbour, but it was clear that it was far too small to be used as a base for two armies; no one had imagined from the maps that it was only a tiny land-locked pool. General Canrobert, who had now taken over from the dying Marshal, offered Lord Raglan the choice, either to continue in his agreed place on the left of the line, or to keep Balaclava, and take the right of the line. Raglan, badly advised by Sir Edmund Lyons, made the wrong decision, he chose Balaclava, not realizing that the two western bays, Kamiesh and Kazach, offered far better facilities as supply ports.

More than that, he committed the British army to the defence of the right flank, in addition to the impending attack on Sevastopol. It was to prove, in the end, a decision for which the army was to pay a terrible price. The French marched westwards, into the south-western corner of the Chersonese. The British 4th Division, left behind on the Belbek, was brought up on to the heights by the pass on the Woronzov Road. On 27 September the allies were approaching the outskirts of Sevastopol. St Arnaud was carried on board ship on the following day, and died at sea on 29 September.

In Sevastopol, the garrison awaited the attack. Colonel Todleben, backed by Admiral Kornilov, set troops and civilians to work day and night to strengthen the defences, and to haul up guns and ammunition into the fortifications.

On 28 and 29 September the allies continued to reconnoitre. The defences grew stronger every hour but still no attack was made. Day after day went by; a week of October passed. Then on the morning of 10 October, a fortnight after the first allied reconnaissance, the watchers in the Russian defences saw a long thin line of dug earth in front of the French positions—the allies had 'broken ground' and thrown up their first parallel; Sevastopol was to be attacked by formal siege. The relief of the defenders was unbounded; the allies had lost another chance.

The causes of this fatal delay were once again the hesitation of the French and more bad advice from Sir John Burgoyne. Lord Raglan and Sir Edmund Lyons were both in favour of immediate attack. Sir John Burgoyne insisted that the defence first be reduced by heavy artillery. He said that the assault would be slaughtered by fire from the warships in the harbour, and that the ravines, with which the south side of Sevastopol is seamed, would hopelessly entangle the attackers. (He had previously argued that these ravines would be an advantage when he was championing the south side attack against the direct approach to the Star Fort.) He also argued that an immediate assault would cost the allies *at least 500 men*.

Lord Raglan at first rejected his advice, and went to the French with a plan for an immediate attack, which Canrobert refused. Sir George Cathcart, on the heights above the eastern approach to the city, looked down on the round tower of the Malakov and the ramparts of the Redan, and wrote to Lord Raglan, 'I am sure I could walk into it, with scarcely the loss of a man, at night or an hour before daybreak . . . we could leave our packs and run into it even in open day, only risking a few shots while we passed the redoubt. We see people walking about the streets in great consternation . . .'

However, he was not to have his chance to walk over 'the low park wall', which formed the fortifications in front of him. Caution prevailed; the decision was taken first to land the siege artillery, and then, inevitably, as the siege artillery could not be brought within range without the construction of proper works, to open a formal siege.

The Chersonese, a rough triangle pointing westwards, is bounded on the north by the landlocked Sevastopol Harbour, at the head of which the Chernaya flows in from the south-east. The eastern boundary of the peninsula is formed by a long escarpment—the Sapouné Heights, pierced by two passes only—the metalled Woronzov Road (leading to Prince Woronzov's villa near Yalta) and at the southern end of the heights The Col, through which ran a steeper and more difficult road leading from the west end of Sevastopol to Balaclava. There were three main crossings of the Chernaya, one near its mouth at the Old Greek Bridge (also called the Inkerman Bridge), the second at the Traktir* Bridge north-east of Balaclava, the third at Chorgun, two miles upstream of the Traktir Bridge. The Woronzov Road ran down from the heights, into a wide valley north of Balaclava, on a ridge, known as the Causeway Heights, which ran east and west, dividing the valley into two sections—the North Valley and the South Valley.

Balaclava was flanked by hills on either side, and was guarded from the north by a small hill at the village of Kadikoi. The North Valley was overlooked on the north side by the Fediukine Heights, through which narrow defiles led to the Traktir Bridge and to Chorgun. Beyond the Chernaya, the ground rose steeply to the Ruins of the Old City of Inkerman, and the Mackenzie Heights.

The Sevastopol plateau, sometimes called the Upland, was intersected by deep ravines, radiating like the spokes of a wheel from the centre of the city; at the point where these ravines reached the harbour, they formed inlets. Reading from east to west, the sequence was as follows: the Careenage

*traktir — inn.

Ravine, known in its upper part as Victoria Ravine, running into the Careenage Creek, where ships could be beached to have the fouling removed from their bottoms; the Dockyard or Middle Ravine, running down to the Dockyard or Ship Bay; the Woronzov Ravine, in which ran the Woronzov Road, and the Picquet House Ravine, both running down to the head of the inner harbour or Dockyard Creek; and lastly the Quarantine Ravine, running into Quarantine Bay to the west of the town. Between these ravines stood ridges on which the main landward defences were sited. These ridges— reading from east to west again, were: the Inkerman Ridge, Victoria Ridge, the Woronzov Height, Green Hill, and to the west, Mount Rodolphe. (See Maps pp. 63, 84, 103.)

The town was divided into two by the Dockyard Creek, the area to the east being called the Karabelnaya or Karabel Suburb. This part of the town was covered originally only by a single round tower—the Malakov. Later the works were developed into a complex containing the Little Redan, the Malakov, and the Great Redan—the first two covering the Victoria Ridge and the last the Woronzov Height and the ravines between.

Protecting the approaches to the head of the Dockyard Creek the Russians later built three main works—the Barrack Battery, the Strand Battery at the water's edge, and the Garden Battery. The Barrack and Garden batteries were mutually supporting.

To the west of the Dockyard Creek lay the Old Town, guarded at first by a stone fort on the southern edge of the town, in front of which was later constructed the Flagstaff Bastion—the French called it *Bastion du Mât*—the Central Bastion, and the Quarantine Bastion, linked to the Artillery Fort, overlooking Artillery Bay.

The seaward defences were very strong. On the north side the entrance to the harbour was protected by Fort Constantine, on the south side by the Quarantine Sea Fort and Fort Alexander. Once inside the harbour, an attacker would find himself between Fort Michael and Fort Catherine to the north, and Fort Nicholas and Fort Paul at the entrance to the Dockyard Creek. Numerous other batteries were constructed later.

The garrison at the time of the arrival of the allies was only some 16,000 strong, all militia and sailors, excepting one regular battalion of the Tarutin regiment. Todleben, in his memoirs, is positive that the allies could have taken Sevastopol either from the north or the south, had they only attempted to do so immediately on their arrival.

The allied armies were divided by the Picquet House Ravine—the French siege corps (3rd and 4th Divisions under Forey), faced the Old Town fortifications—the Flagstaff, Central and Quarantine Bastions, while the British looked down on the Malakov and the two Redans and faced towards the Chernaya on the Sapouné Heights. On their southern flank, the French Corps of Observation (1st and 2nd Divisions under Canrobert) occupied the Sapouné Heights above Balaclava. (See Map p. 117.)

The Malakov, originally a simple round tower, was rapidly being concealed behind massive earthworks, faced by a bare sloping *glacis*; a new semi-circular battery was built round the tower; entrenchments connected it with the Redans on each side. Ships were sited in the creeks where their fire could rake the ravines; a signalling system was organized. By the evening of 29 September, the defences were in enough order to receive an attack. On that day the Russian army reappeared on the North Side, reinforced by 10,000 new troops. After a council of war with Kornilov and Todleben, now promoted to General, Prince Menshikov held to his view that the army should not enter Sevastopol, but should operate from north of the Chernaya, keeping open communications with the mainland of Russia, and preventing the allies from investing Sevastopol. The threat to the open eastern flank would also force the allies to use troops in that quarter, rather than to attack Sevastopol.

Admiral Kornilov, however, insisted that the garrison alone could not continue to hold Sevastopol, and Prince

Menshikov was eventually persuaded to increase the garrison by another twelve battalions, bringing up the strength on 6 October to about 38,000.

Thus the allies, by their lack of drive and offensive spirit, allowed the beaten Russian army to recover its balance, and the garrison of Sevastopol to strengthen the defences on the landward side from a total of 172 guns to 341, firing nearly three times the weight of shot. Against this strength the allies had assembled 126 guns, including 18 heavy mortars; of these guns, 53 were French and 73 British. Opposite the Malakov on Victoria Ridge was a Lancaster battery; on the Woronzov Height, was the British Right Attack (Chapman's Battery of 26 guns); on Green Hill, facing the Redan and the east side of the Flagstaff Bastion, was the British Left Attack (Gordon's Battery of 41 guns). The French sited 49 guns on Mount Rodolphe facing the Central Bastion and the west side of the Flagstaff Bastion. At 6.30 am on 17 October, the cannonade began, at a signal fired from Mount Rodolphe.

A naval bombardment had been planned to begin at the same time but at 10.30 pm on the previous night Admiral Dundas heard that Admiral Hamelin did not intend to open fire till 10 am. Next morning, worse was to come; Admiral Hamelin arrived on board Dundas's flagship with a complete change of plan. Instead of the fleets carrying out the bombardment in motion, they were to be anchored off the forts— the French opposing the Quarantine Sea Fort, the British attacking Fort Constantine and its neighbouring batteries— the Wasp and the Telegraph Battery. Dundas, flabbergasted, had no choice but to accept the new plan, which took until the early afternoon to organize.

By this time the Russians had scored a hit on a magazine in the French batteries on Mount Rodolphe. The enormous explosion caused the French to lose heart; their batteries ceased fire for the rest of the day. The British were more successful, especially against the Redan, which was reduced to rubble, and finally blown up. No assault was made, however,

6

since Lord Raglan had agreed with Canrobert that the two armies should attack together. As no French attack was forthcoming, the British were forced to hold back. Thus, the last easy chance of invading Sevastopol was lost.

The naval bombardment achieved little. The French line was too far out to sea to do much damage to the powerful Quarantine Fort; the British, by good reconnaissance, got into a position from which they could engage Fort Constantine from the rear; all the guns in the open on the top of the fort were knocked out, but those in casemates on the lower tiers were unaffected. The Russian Telegraph Battery, firing from the top of the cliff, did so much damage to the British ships that they were eventually forced to withdraw.

During the day, Admiral Kornilov, touring the front, was killed in the Malakov. The loss of this popular and dynamic man was a great blow to the Russians. Kornilov and Todleben had together saved the city; the initiative was now to pass to the Russians.

CHAPTER VIII

The Defence of Balaclava

On the morning of 18 October, while Lord Raglan was watching the British artillery bombarding the Redan for the second day, news was brought to him which sent him cantering at once to the Sapouné Heights. A large Russian force was seen marching on a ridge above Chorgun. Up to this time patrols had clashed in the valley of the Chernaya, but there had been as yet no serious threat to the eastern flank.

The defences on that side now consisted of an inner line round Balaclava, taking in the high ground west of the harbour, manned by Royal Marines (and renamed the Marine Heights), and Kadikoi, defended by the 93rd Regiment. An outer line was established on the Causeway Heights, where six redoubts had been dug—the easternmost, No 1, on 'Canrobert's Hill' a small detached feature—the remainder being strung along the heights on the line of the Woronzov Road. These redoubts were manned by Turks, supported by British 12-pounder guns from the fleet and supervised by an artillery NCO in each redoubt.

The Cavalry Division was encamped on the south side of the Causeway Heights, close under No 6 redoubt. Above, on the Sapouné Heights, lay Bosquet's 'corps of observation', from the Woronzov Road to The Col. Between The Col and the sea, Canrobert's Turkish battalions were encamped. Sir Colin Campbell was in command of the defences, but the Cavalry Division was unfortunately not put under his control.

Prince Menshikov had assembled, in the Chorgun area, a force of 17 infantry battalions, 30 squadrons of cavalry and 64 guns, under the command of General Liprandi, supported

73

by a separate force of 8 battalions, 4 squadrons of cavalry and 14 guns, under General Jabrokritski.

Liprandi's intention was to capture the outer line of defence and the position at Kadikoi covering the exit from Balaclava. The Russian force was divided into three columns; the left, under General Gribbé, was to emerge from the Baidar Valley, to the east, and capture the Kamara Heights; the centre, under General Semiakin, was to advance from Chorgun, directed on Redoubts No 1 and 2; while the right, under Col Scudery, was to cross the Traktir Bridge, and capture Redoubt No 3, named the 'Arab Tabia'. The cavalry, under General Ryjov, was to enter the North Valley from the north-east, while Jabrokritski's force was to follow Scudery across the Traktir Bridge and hold the Fediukine Heights.

A spy brought this plan to the Turkish Brigade commander, on 24 October. Both Lord Lucan and Sir Colin Campbell were impressed by the importance of his message, which they passed on to Lord Raglan. His only comment was, 'Very well'. Probably influenced by a false report a few days before, he took no further action.

At 5 am on 25 October, the Russians advanced, occupied the Kamara Heights, placed 30 guns in battery, and opened fire on Canrobert's Hill. Liprandi's opening moves went according to plan. The Azov Brigade captured Canrobert's Hill, the Ukraine Brigade took Redoubt No 2, the Odessa Brigade routed the Turks from the Arab Tabia and Redoubt No 4, and Jabrokritski's force was beginning to establish itself on the Fediukine Heights, screened by skirmishers from the Foot Cossacks and Rifles.

In reply Lord Lucan advanced with the Heavy Brigade, threatening, but without effect, the Russian infantry advance. He then drew off to the west end of the Causeway Heights, where he was in a good position to support Sir Colin Campbell.

Lord Raglan ordered the 1st and 4th Divisions to start marching to the defence of Balaclava, and alerted the 3rd Division against a possible sortie from Sevastopol. The

1st Division eventually descended by the Woronzov Road and the 4th Division by The Col, after a somewhat delayed start, due to the troops being at breakfast after a night in the trenches.

Canrobert despatched two infantry brigades, under Vinoy and Espinasse, and two cavalry regiments of Chasseurs d'Afrique, under d'Allonville, to the foot of the heights.

Lord Raglan then ordered Lord Lucan to move the cavalry more to the north, on the left of Redoubt No 6; this move left open the front for the advance of Ryjov's cavalry, which was now drawn up between the Fediukine Heights and the Causeway.

As the Turks fled from the redoubts (rifling the British cavalry camp on their way) only Sir Colin Campbell's little force of the 93rd, one field battery, two heavy guns, two other battalions of Turks, and 100 invalids under Col Daveney, stood between the Russians and the harbour.

Liprandi, however, had no intention of trying to seize Balaclava. According to Todleben, his aim was to destroy an 'artillery park' near Kadikoi. Whatever the intention, Ryjov's cavalry now advanced in a huge mass from which four squadrons were soon detached, heading for Kadikoi. Their arrival was too much for the two Turkish battalions, who turned and ran. The 93rd, in line two-deep, awaiting the charge, opened fire when the Russian cavalry came within long range. At a second volley the Russians, with little damage done to their ranks, wheeled off to their left, as if to outflank the 93rd. Colin Campbell shifted his right-hand company to meet the threat; after a third volley the Russians wheeled again and retreated. This easy victory has ever since been referred to as the 'Thin Red Line' and is generally represented in pictures as a determined cavalry attack being beaten off at close quarters.

The main body of the Russian cavalry then crossed the Causeway Heights, where they were seen by the Heavy Brigade, which was moving slowly, at Lord Raglan's orders, back to the support of the 93rd.

Scarlett, at the head of the Heavy Brigade, wheeled to the left, carefully dressed the line, and charged uphill at the trot, through the entangling wreckage of the Light Brigade camp. The Heavy Brigade, some 600 strong, was swallowed up in a mass of nearly 3,000 Russians. The Greys, Inniskillings and 5th Dragoon Guards met the Russian front head-on, while the Royals and the 4th Dragoon Guards took the enemy on the western flank. Incredibly, the redcoats hacked their way through the grey enemy masses, until the Russian force started to sway and melt. Scarlett cut his way right through and out of the enemy's left flank.

Throughout this struggle, the regiments of the Light Brigade, under the Earl of Cardigan, sat motionless, a few hundred yards away, and made no move to support their comrades. Cardigan remained inactive because he thought Lucan had put him into position with orders to stay there. Lucan thought he had ordered Cardigan to 'attack anything and everything . . . within reach'; but mutual relations between the two men were such that misunderstanding was inevitable. Cardigan's commanding officers urged him to allow a charge, but he firmly refused. The enemy cavalry straggled away to the north-east, unmolested, to reform in the shelter of their guns at the east end of the North Valley.

Meanwhile, at the redoubts, the Russians were taking steps to carry away the captured guns. Lord Raglan drafted a message to Lord Lucan, his famous 'fourth order', 'Lord Raglan wishes the cavalry to advance rapidly to the front, follow the enemy and try to prevent the enemy carrying away the guns. Troop horse artillery may accompany. French cavalry is on your left. Immediate.'

Airey signed the message, and Raglan told him to send it with Nolan, since it was urgent. Nolan, a wonderful horseman, chafing with fury at the inaction of the cavalry since the first hours of the landing, descended the heights at a breakneck gallop and handed the message to the man he detested and whom he had nicknamed 'Lord Look-on'. Down in the valley the redoubts were no longer visible. Lucan queried the order, 'Attack, Sir, attack what? What guns, sir?' 'There, my Lord, is your enemy; there are your guns', and Nolan pointed not towards the redoubts, but up the valley to the batteries, behind which the Russian cavalry had reformed.

Thus the fate of the Light Brigade was determined. Lord Cardigan, after querying the order without success, led the Light Brigade quietly off at a trot; Lucan remained, to follow with the Heavy Brigade. The Light Brigade was formed thus, with a front line 200 yards wide, and 400 yards between successive lines:

Nolan, who was riding with the 17th, rode out to Lord Cardigan, shouting and waving his sword, much to his Lordship's disgust; however, the first enemy shell hit Nolan and killed him. The general opinion, for which there is little real evidence, is that Nolan was trying to redirect the brigade, when it became apparent that Lord Cardigan was heading for the wrong objective. Sgt.-Major Nunnerly, of the 17th, riding on the right of his regiment, and therefore very near Nolan, declared that his shout sounded like 'threes right', and in fact some of his men started to obey the order, until they were checked.

The Light Brigade, now under fire from both the Fediukine Heights and the Causeway, overran the guns and engaged the enemy cavalry beyond. Once again, in a confused struggle, the Russian cavalry failed, and were pushed back into the mouth of the gorge leading to the Chorgun crossings. The small numbers of Light Brigade survivors who had passed the guns, reformed into scattered groups, and began to return, to find their way blocked by Jeropkine's Lancers, who had advanced from either flank to cut off their retreat. However, even these fresh troops, incapable of anything but clumsy and limited manœuvre, allowed the British to edge their way past them back to safety. Pressure from the Fediukine Heights was relieved by an effective charge by d'Allonville's Chasseurs d'Afrique, launched by General Morris, the French cavalry commander.

The Heavy Brigade, following up at a distance, came under fire once the fourth redoubt had been passed. Lord Lucan, seeing that the Light Brigade was irretrievably lost, decided not to throw the Heavy Brigade after it, and halted the advance.

Liprandi had consolidated the area from the first to the third redoubts so effectively that when the Duke of Cambridge and Lord Cathcart eventually arrived with their divisions, Sir Colin Campbell advised against an attack to recapture the redoubts. The failure of the Turks under fire and the loss of the Light Brigade must have made it clear to Lord Raglan that even if he succeeded in recapturing the Causeway Heights he would have to withdraw infantry from the attack on Sevastopol in order to hold them. Thus the Russians were left in possession of the first three redoubts and of the Woronzov Road.

This last loss is generally quoted as a main cause of the allied administrative difficulties during the winter. But the Woronzov Road did not pass nearer than two miles to Balaclava, to which it was linked only by a rough track through Kadikoi. Pemberton Baring, in his excellent book *Battles of the Crimean War*, quotes a Capt Montgomery of the 49th as saying that the 'Woronzov road was never used for the transport of guns . . . a part . . . was used for the transport of ammunition, but we had to cross the mud in the open country to get to this mile of road'.

In any case, the Russians withdrew beyond the Chernaya early in December, 1854, leaving the road to the British— who continued to use The Col. The 'vital Woronzov road' is a myth perpetuated by W. H. Russell, *The Times* correspondent, and by those who needed an excuse for administrative failure.

The recriminations after Balaclava lasted for years. Lord Cardigan, who had led the charge so bravely, took no further part in the battle after he had passed through the line of guns. He rode quietly back alone, without attempting either to rally the remnants of the front line, or to find and take control of the supporting regiments, which had gone slightly astray in the general confusion. He did not, as is generally believed, return to his yacht immediately but slept the night on the battlefield. He left the Crimea for reasons of ill-health not long after the battle, and was received as a hero in Britain. But he overplayed his hand, antagonizing many officers who had taken part in the charge, and he became involved in long and unsuccessful litigation. Nevertheless, he was awarded the KCB and held the post of Inspector-General of Cavalry until 1860.

Lord Lucan, who was accused by Lord Raglan of losing the Light Brigade, took exception to the wording of Raglan's dispatch on the battle. He wrote to Raglan asking that his side of the matter be put forward. Raglan then sent Airey to ask Lucan to withdraw his letter; this Lucan refused to do, so Raglan forwarded the letter to the Horse Guards. The Secretary of State for War backed Raglan, with the result that Lucan was ordered to resign his command of the Cavalry Division. He then asked for a court-martial, a request which was not granted.

One cannot help feeling sorry for Lucan, who had never received much support from Lord Raglan. At Scutari it was Lord Cardigan who had been allowed to take charge of the cavalry force embarking for Varna, while Lucan was left behind. He had to fight hard not to be left behind again when the expedition left for the Crimea. He was allowed no scope in the handling of his cavalry before or after the Alma. Finally at Balaclava he was the victim of some very vague orders, delivered by an insubordinate ADC, who gave him an entirely wrong impression.

Admittedly he was out of date, arrogant, and obstinate, and his relations with Cardigan were impossible. But it was Lord Raglan who should have resolved this situation, by the removal of one or other of the two incompatibles, instead of mildly tolerating a state of affairs which was bound to lead to inefficiency. Raglan must bear much of the blame for the casualties at Balaclava; a commander is only as good as the orders he transmits to his troops. However sound his tactics, if he cannot make known his intentions clearly, he will fail; and the first place in which he must look for the cause of failure is in himself. He must constantly ask himself whether or not he made himself clear. He must bear the responsibility for the failure of his own staff to interpret his intentions to the troops, and for the failure of the troops to carry out his intentions. Raglan's orders were vague; Airey's written interpretations were no better; Nolan's method of delivery of the message was inexcusable; Lucan was too inflexible and blinkered to anticipate his commander's real intentions; Cardigan had no choice but to obey.

Disastrous as the charge seemed to be, the casualties according to Kinglake, out of a strength of 673, amounted to 113 killed, 134 wounded and 15 taken prisoner, a surprisingly small figure; it was the loss of 475 horses that crippled the brigade as a fighting force, in a campaign where there was anyway to be little further use for cavalry. If only Lord Cardigan had succeeded either in giving support to the Heavy Brigade, or in rallying the Light Brigade, after the Charge, and had made a cohesive move against the demoralized Russian cavalry, Balaclava could have been turned into a victory. As it was, the failure stunned the allied infantry into inactivity, and gave heart to the Russian armies both inside and outside Sevastopol.

CHAPTER IX

The Russian Offensive at Inkerman

The day after Balaclava, Sunday 26 October, the Russians staged a minor attack on the British 2nd Division. The main British position was on the Home Ridge,* with a line of outpost picquets, at company strength, stretching from the Kitspur and the Inkerman Tusk, through the Barrier (the road-block on the post-road running from the Inkerman Bridge through the Home Ridge) across the front of Shell Hill,* thence covering the front of the Lancaster battery on Victoria Ridge, and the British siege works.

Col Federov, with six battalions and four guns, moved out by road from the Karabel suburb, crossed the Careenage Ravine by the viaduct and advanced on Shell Hill, where his force was engaged by the picquet line. At first the outposts held firm, and de Lacy Evans refused to commit any further strength to their aid; when the Russian force eventually broke through, it was smashed by artillery fire from Home Ridge. Another Russian column, about 700 strong, advancing under cover of the Careenage Ravine, was met and held by a small party of guards under Capt Goodlake, who later won the VC. The Russians lost 270 killed and wounded at this 'Little Inkerman'—the British, about 100. De Lacy Evans having fallen heavily from his horse, was forced to hand over command of the 2nd Division to Brigadier-General Pennefather.

*Home Ridge was 636 feet above sea level, Shell Hill 588 feet. Shell Hill is often depicted as dominating Home Ridge, but it did not. Raglan was criticized for not occupying Shell Hill, but troops on it could have easily been cut off.

On the same day, Cathcart's 'dormant commission' was cancelled at Lord Raglan's request; the Commander-in-Chief felt that its operation would have been invidious to Sir George Brown.

In the week that followed, the Russians built up their strength in the Chernaya valley, and closed up their picquet lines facing the defences of Balaclava. The Russian strength was now so greatly increased that it was the allies who were in danger of being besieged in the Chersonese: 40,000 French and 25,000 British now faced 120,000 Russians. Sevastopol was not 'invested'; the Russians had access not only by the road to the east, but also by crossing the harbour from the north side.

The warning of 'Little Inkerman' was not taken. No new dispositions were made on the British front, and few new defences were prepared. To shelter the guns on Home Ridge, a shallow work was dug (against Burgoyne's advice); the troops named it 'Herbert's Folly'.

On the Kitspur a two-gun battery was built, as a reply to a single gun which was firing from the Ruins of Inkerman across the valley. By 4 November the guns had been withdrawn and the earthworks abandoned. This was the 'Sandbag Battery', untenable by infantry, being nine feet deep, without firesteps. In the coming fight it was to be a great embarrassment to both sides.

The whole of the front was covered with dense oak scrub, about the height of a man. No effort was made to clear fields of fire in front of Home Ridge, where some guns were actually touching the edge of the scrub.

The 2nd Division still lay in camp on Home Ridge, behind their screen of outposts. In the 1st Division, the Guards' camp was near the windmill on the Post Road, with picquets overlooking the Chernaya Valley, and at the head of the Wellway—a branch of the Careenage Ravine which debouched near the rear of 2nd Division's Camp. The Highland Brigade, the other half of the 1st Division, was at Balaclava.

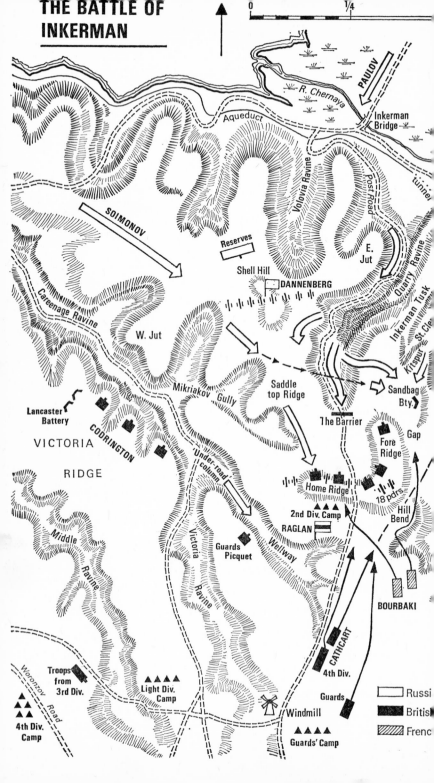

THE BATTLE OF
INKERMAN

0   1/4

PAULOV

R. Chernaya

Aqueduct

Inkerman
Bridge

Tunnel

SOIMONOV

Volovia Ravine

Post Road

Reserves

E.
Jut

Shell Hill

DANNENBERG

Quarry Ravine

Carenage Ravine

Inkerman Tusk

W. Jut

St. Cle

Mikriakov Gully

Krispur

Saddle
top Ridge

Sandbag
Bty.

Lancaster
Battery

CODRINGTON

The Barrier

Gap

VICTORIA

Fore
Ridge

RIDGE

Under-road
column

18 pdrs

Home Ridge

Hill
Bend

2nd Div. Camp

RAGLAN

Middle
Ravine

Victoria Ravine

Guards
Picquet

Weltway

BOURBAKI

Woronzov
Road

Troops
from
3rd Div.

Light Div.
Camp

CATHCART

4th Div.

4th Div.
Camp

Windmill

Guards

Guards' Camp

Russi

Britis

Frenc

The 4th and 3rd Divisions' camps extended the same line westwards towards the French positions. The Light Brigade, or what was left of it, was in support of the Guards' position, while the Heavy Brigade was camped on The Col near British headquarters, ready for action either on the plateau, or in defence of Balaclava.

The French preparations for attack on the Flagstaff Bastion were nearly complete. The Russian attack was designed as a 'spoiling' operation.

Prince Menshikov's plan was for a double-headed advance by General Soimonov's army of 19,000 men from Sevastopol, and General Paulov's army of 16,000 men from the Mackenzie Heights. Soimonov was to advance up to the Western Jut* of Shell Hill, and there establish his artillery. Paulov's force was to descend from the Mackenzie Heights, cross the Inkerman Bridge (which had been demolished, and was now to be rebuilt by sailors), and then advance by the Quarry Ravine, directed on the East Jut* of Shell Hill and on the Barrier.

General Gorchakov, facing Balaclava with an army of 22,000, was to demonstrate against the Sapouné Heights, in order to pin down allied forces on the right flank.

When Soimonov and Paulov were united on Shell Hill, General Dannenberg was to assume command, in a drive southwards towards the windmill on the Woronzov Road. When the troops reached this point, Gorchakov was to attack from the east, to complete the destruction of the British Army.

Dannenberg rightly objected to the plan, on the grounds that the area of Shell Hill and Saddle-top Ridge, which linked it to Home Ridge, was too constricted for the forces involved. He suggested that Soimonov's army should advance *west* of the Careenage Ravine, on the Victoria Ridge. Had this suggestion been adopted, the Russians would probably have won the battle. The idea seems to have been accepted, but no executive orders to put it into effect were

*Kinglake's phrase.

issued, Soimonov persisting wilfully with the original plan.

In preparation for the battle, Menshikov ordered Liprandi to demonstrate against Balaclava on 2 November. Lord Raglan had contemplated abandoning the port, on Sir Edmund Lyons's advice, but Mr Filder, the Commissary General, was adamant that he could not supply the army without it. Sailors were landed to strengthen the garrison, a battleship was stationed in the harbour and French and Turkish troops were added to the Highland Brigade in the defence.

Rumours of the impending attack reached England from Russia even before they reached the Crimea, and had been transmitted in many letters from home. Kinglake says that 'the dutiful Muscovite soldier was enraptured with the tidings that two of the Imperial Princes had resolved to come and share the peril and glory of the approaching fight'. They arrived in a small yellow carriage which was spotted by Pennefather on 4 November, on reconnaissance on Shell Hill. Special patrols were sent to the Inkerman Tusk to report any new movements, but nothing was seen except large numbers of sheep.

The Russians began to move at 2 am on Sunday 5 November; the rumbling of the artillery was clearly heard by the forward picquets, but was mistaken for carts going to market. The battle began at 5.45 am, on a morning of dense fog, when the Russian forces encountered the outlying picquets.

The battle of Inkerman was so complicated and so difficult to follow, that the main events of it are shown in tabulated form below. Times are approximate, as few accurate records were kept. The division into periods is Kinglake's.

1. The Allied fleet leaves Varna for the invasion of the Crimea (*Illustrated London News*)

2. The inner defences of Balaclava, from the mound at Kadikoi. In the foreground Highlanders and artillerymen stand beside a field gun and a howitzer. Beyond, the fortifications on the Marine Heights; on the right, Balaclava and the railway. Drawn in 1855, when administration troubles were over.

Fediukine Heights
Home Ridge
Inkerman Heights   Shell Hill
Sevastopol Harbour   Ruins of Inkerman
Tractir Bridge   Russian redoubts
Russian redoubts
Chorgun
Mackenzie's Farm
Karlovka

3. A view of the valley of the Chernaya from the Sardinian positions overlooking Chorgun. Above Chorgun on the distant skyline is Mackenzie's Farm, and the road leading to Bakchi Serai.

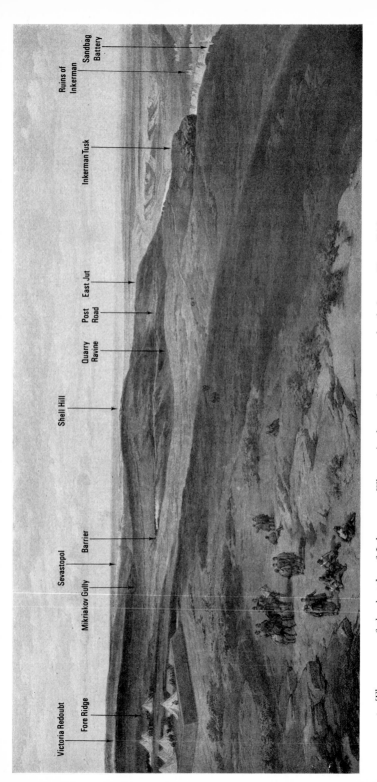

4. The scene of the battle of Inkerman. The redoubts and tents on the left, on Fore Ridge, were not there at the time of the battle. In the foreground is 'The Gap' between the Sandbag Battery and Fore Ridge.

Victoria Redoubt — Fore Ridge — Mikriakov Gully — Sevastopol — Barrier — Shell Hill — Quarry Ravine — Post Road — East Jut — Inkerman Tusk — Ruins of Inkerman — Sandbag Battery

5. A sketch of the Sandbag Battery made the morning after the Battle of Inkerman by an *Illustrated London News* correspondent.

6. Captain Peel and Commander Burnet of the Naval Brigade stand above a 68-pounder Lancaster in the Diamond Battery on Victoria Ridge. Note the lanyard leading to the friction-tube with which the gun was fired, the primitive back-sight, rammers and sponges, charges in cylindrical boxes and a round of grape in the left foreground. On the wooden platform on which the gun recoiled lies what looks like a round shot and, nearer the muzzle, a shell.

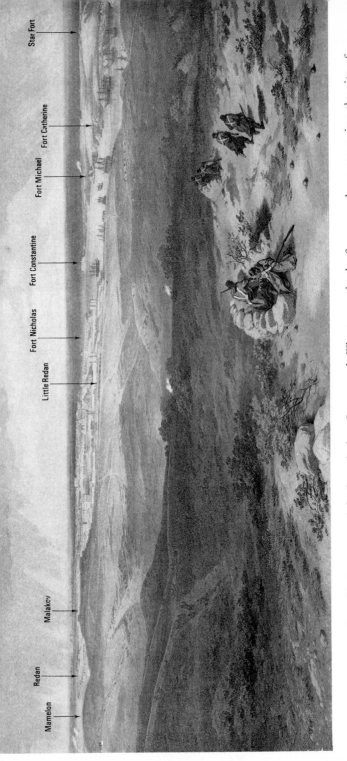

Star Fort
Fort Catherine
Fort Michael
Fort Constantine
Fort Nicholas
Little Redan
Malakov
Redan
Mamelon

7. View of the Allied extreme right front before Sevastopol. The troops in the foreground are occupying the site of the Russian 'White Works'. Note how the Russian left flank is covered by warships in the harbour.

8. View from Gordon's Battery, in the British Right Attack. In the foreground are 10" and 13" mortars; on the right are a variety of siege guns.

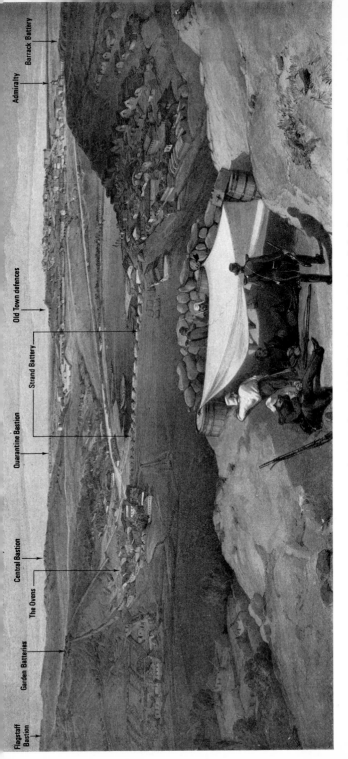

Flagstaff Bastion   Garden Batteries   The Ovens   Central Bastion   Quarantine Bastion   Strand Battery   Old Town defences   Admiralty   Barrack Battery

9. View of the head of the Dockyard Creek from the British Left Attack. In the right foreground the Woronzov road is covered by the Barrack Battery on the hill, and the Strand Battery at the water's edge. Note how the approaches to the Old Town, behind the Flagstaff Bastion, can be swept by fire from the Barrack Battery.

Old Town defences · Karabelnaya · Shell Hill · Malakov · Home Ridge · Mamelon · Garden Batteries · Redan · Flagstaff Bastion

10. View from the Central Bastion after the capture of Sevastopol. This picture gives a good impression of the scale of Todleben's fortifications, all improvised out of earth, timber, sandbags, gabions, with a gun to every few yards of front.

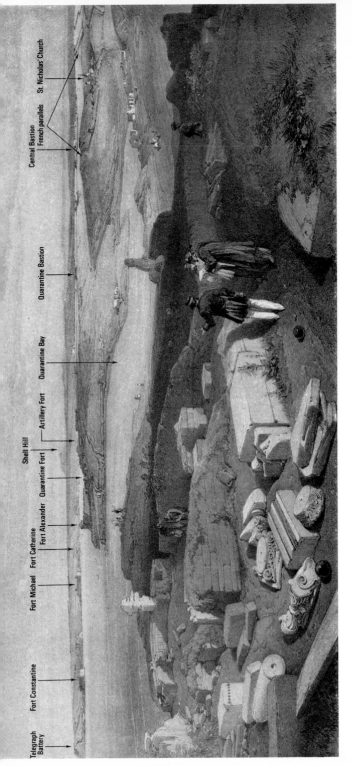

Telegraph Battery · Fort Constantine · Fort Michael · Fort Catherine · Fort Alexander · Quarantine Fort · Shell Hill · Artillery Fort · Quarantine Bay · Quarantine Bastion · Central Bastion · French parallels · St. Nicholas' Church

11. The extreme left of the French front. Although there was fierce fighting in the area of the Quarantine Cemetery of St. Nicholas, the open approaches across the Quarantine Ravine prevented any serious threat to the Russians on this flank.

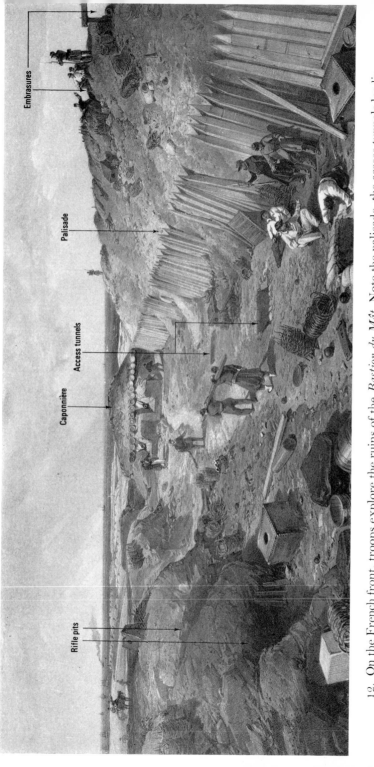

12. On the French front, troops explore the ruins of the *Bastion du Mât*. Note the palisade, the access tunnels leading down from the ditch, rifle pits in the front wall of the ditch, and the '*caponnière*' or pill-box covering the ditch. Among the debris are *gabions* —the wickerwork cylinders, and water-tanks, possibly used as improvised armour-plate.

Embrasures

Palisade

Access tunnels

Caponnière

Rifle pits

Mamelon

Malakov

Gervais Battery

British 5th parallel

Redan

Barrack Battery

13. Sevastopol in flames, on the evening of 9 September, 1855. The main allied effort was made against the Malakov, right centre, and the Redan—above which the British flag flies. On the opposite slope, in sunlight, lies the British Right Attack—third, fourth and fifth parallels. Troops return from the front with firewood collected from the ruins. On the near side of the Woronzov ravine lie the parallels of the British Left Attack.

Tractir Bridge **Mackenzie Heights** **Aqueduct Bridge**

14. The battle of the Chernaya. The Russian attack is being repulsed from the slopes of the Fediukine Heights on the left. In the centre, the main column withdraws over the Traktir Bridge; on the right Zouaves defend the bridge over the Aqueduct. In the distance Russian guns fire from the Mackenzie Heights.

15. The city of Kars from the south-west. On the right, the Karadagh Heights; left centre, the citadel, with the Tachmasb Heights beyond to the left. The river bends through the gorge to the left of the citadel. The tower at the extreme left is the Vassif Pasha Tabia.

16. Naval ingenuity in the Sea of Azov—the *Lady Nancy* raft drawing only 20 inches, carries a 32-pounder gun into the shallow waters of Taganrog. She is accompanied by a Whaler mounting a Congreve Rocket launcher.

(Illustrated London News)

THE BATTLE OF INKERMAN

First period
0545–0730

RUSSIAN	ALLIED
Soimonov's army (19,000) with 8 bns, Tomsk and Kolivansk regts leading, and 22 heavy 12 pdr guns advances on spine of Mt Inkerman towards Shell Hill, with 4 Katerinburg bns in support.	Troop movements heard by Codrington's force on Victoria Ridge overlooking Careenage Ravine. Codrington alerts Sir George Brown, who informs Lord Raglan.
First contact with British picquets on Shell Hill. Picquets are driven back. Soimonov establishes 22 guns on West Jut of Shell Hill, and engages the ground behind Home Ridge.	Picquet's firing heard. Pennefather calls troops to arms and forms up on Home Ridge. Artillery on Home Ridge opens fire into the mist.
	Pennefather, rather than adopting a reverse slope position behind Home Ridge (which Evans would have done) elects to 'feed the picquets' by pushing forward small bodies of men into the brushwood to engage the enemy—30th and 41st under Adams, with half 49th (Bellairs) to the right, half 49th (Dalton) and 47th (Fordyce) to left towards Mikriakov Gully. Most of 2nd Div is thus moved forward off Home Ridge.
Soimonov sends a strong reconnaissance to Mikriakov Gully which is met by 49th under Grant (Dalton killed). Grant yields ground slowly.	

RUSSIAN	ALLIED
0700 An 'Under-Road Column' of 100 Katerinburg Riflemen advances up the Careenage Ravine towards the Wellway.	Lord Raglan arrives at Home Ridge and sends a message for two 18 pdrs of the siege artillery to be brought up. The message miscarries (to the commander of the batteries on Home Ridge) who is fully occupied, and replies 'impossible'. The message is redirected to the artillery park. The following movements are also in train—not necessarily at Raglan's orders, but partly on the initiative of the commanders themselves: Cathcart's 4th Division, with 2,300 men and Townsend's battery starts towards the Home Ridge. Sir George Brown with the Light Division sends Buller's Brigade of 650 men to Home Ridge, and Codrington's brigade to strengthen the picquet guarding the Victoria Ridge; England's 3rd Division starts to move north-east and occupy ground vacated by the Light Division, and to watch the centre and left. England subsequently detached various units to the Home Ridge front, but remained in the area of the British siege works himself.

RUSSIAN

On the Balaclava front, Gor-chakov's demonstration is so feeble, that neither Bosquet nor the Duke of Cambridge are deceived.

Soimonov now attacks in strength, skirting the rim of the Mikriakov Gully with some 9,000 men in company columns. One Katerinburg battalion, losing direction, strays across the face of Shell Hill, heading due east.

Paulov's column (16,000)

ALLIED

At the Guards Brigade camp, the Duke of Cambridge orders the Coldstream to man the Sapouné Heights, and leads the Grenadiers and Scots Fusilier Guards towards Pennefather's front.

Bosquet orders two battalions (6th and 7th) with artillery, to move to the windmill. On the way he meets Sir George Brown, and Sir George Cathcart, who tell him they do not need his help! Bosquet returns to the Col, but later sends Brigadier Bourbaki with the same troops towards the area of Home Ridge. Away to the west, near Mount Rodolphe, Prince Napoleon, at Canrobert's orders, starts three battalions marching towards the Inkerman front.

The Light Division reinforcements, under Sir George Brown, reach General Pennefather, whose force now totals 3,600, and 16 guns. They are put into action at the left end of Home Ridge, advance towards the Mikriakov Gully, and are driven back by the weight of Soimonov's advance. Three

RUSSIAN	ALLIES
ascending by the Post Road, approaches the Barrier, four Borodino Regiments leading, in company columns, three up and one back. The Tarutin battalions on their right, halt on the East Jut of Shell Hill until they see the stray Katerinburg battalion moving east; they then follow it. In reserve behind Shell Hill stand 16 battalions (Vladimir, Susdal, Uglitz, Butirsk).	field guns (Townsend) are left unprotected and are captured by the Russians. Paulov's force is met by Col Mauleverer and 200 men of 30th Regiment, at the Barrier; and by Adams with 500 men of the 41st, on the high ground at the base of the Kitspur. The 30th's rifles are damp and will not fire. Mauleverer leads a bayonet charge over the Barrier.
The Under-Road Column appears at the head of the Wellway, in rear of 2nd Division camp, and is driven back by Clifford's charge, and fire from the Grenadier picquet.	General Buller arrives at 2nd Division camp. His ADC, Henry Clifford, sees the Russians in the Wellway and leads a party of 77th Regt against them. Prince Edward of Saxe-Weimar, on the western lip of the Wellway, with a picquet of Grenadiers, engages the Under-Road Column.
One Katerinburg battalion from Soimonov's reserve advances on the Home Ridge by the western slope of Saddle-top.	The 47th (Fordyce) advances to meet and check the Katerinburg battalion.
0730 The remaining Katerinburg battalions attack in force on the rim of the Mikriakov Gully. Two Tomsk and four	The 49th (Grant) holds firm against this attack. 2nd Division troops in the brushwood are out of

RUSSIAN	ALLIED
Kolivansk battalions then attack Home Ridge.	ammunition. The advance of the Kolivansk battalions is met by grape from Turner's battery, fired over their own troops, who are ordered to lie down. Buller orders the 77th (Egerton) to charge the Tomsk Battalions. The charge is successful. Townsend's guns are recaptured.
The Russians break and are driven back to Shell Hill. Soimonov (conspicuous as the only mounted officer on the Russian side), is killed. The Katerinburg battalions, seeing the Tomsk battalions withdrawing, break and run.	Buller is wounded. The withdrawing Russians are pursued with the bayonet.
One Kolivansk battalion strays too far to the left, and threatens Hill Bend, the junction of Home Ridge and Fore Ridge.	This battalion is charged and routed by the 49th (Capt Bellairs).
The stray Katerinburg battalion, which has reached the Russian left, sees the unoccupied Sandbag Battery on the Kitspur, assumes it to be part of the British defences, and followed by the Tarutin Battalions, seizes and occupies the earthwork.	Adams counter-attacks with the 41st and recaptures the Sandbag Battery. The enemy fall back on to the lower ground. Adams succeeds in preventing his troops from following the enemy down.

Thus at the end of the first period, the Russian attacks have been held all along the line. Soimonov's army, with the death of its leader, takes little further part in the battle. The fog lifts, making it easier for the Russians to find their way on unfamiliar ground, but giving advantage to the superior British riflemen.

Second Period
0730–0830

0730 General Dannenberg takes command. Paulov's artillery —now 97 guns, is sited on the forward slope of Shell Hill, on the East Jut.
The Okhotsk, Yakutsk and Selinghinsk battalions advance to capture the Sandbag Battery.

The Russians continue to press for the Sandbag Battery.

ALLIES

Pennefather moves Bellairs and the 49th to the aid of Adams at the Sandbag Battery. Adams is forced to abandon the battery and receives a fatal wound.
Reinforcements begin to arrive: three field batteries, 1,200 men of the Guards, 2,000 of 4th Division, two French battalions under Bourbaki.
The batteries go into action on Fore Ridge, and drive the enemy into the cover of Quarry Ravine.
The Grenadier Guards advance and recapture the Sandbag Battery; the Scots Fusilier Guards repel an attack from St Clements Ravine. The Grenadiers find the Battery untenable and abandon it.
'The Gap' opens between the Sandbag Battery and the Barrier.
The Duke of Cambridge asks Cathcart to fill 'The Gap'; Cathcart refuses. The Duke

RUSSIAN	ALLIES
The Okhotsk Battalions recapture the Sandbag Battery supported by heavy artillery fire, but are again driven out.	of Cambridge and Pennefather try to persuade the French to move into 'The Gap'. The French, drawn up in square, will not move.
	The Grenadiers recapture the Sandbag Battery: and resist a further attack by the Okhotsk.
The Selinghinsk battalions attack from the eastern slopes of the Kitspur.	Cathcart arrives with 4th Division and allots his leading brigade piecemeal to Pennefather. With his second brigade, under Torrens, he declines to fill 'The Gap', but decides to make an outflanking move to the right on the lower slopes of the Kitspur. Airey tries to countermand this plan, and gives Lord Raglan's direct order that Cathcart is to support the Guards.
One Yakutsk battalion crosses to its left to counter Cathcart's outflanking move.	Cathcart disobeys the order, and orders Torrens to attack on the right flank. The Brigade descends the slopes, driving the Russians before it, and follows them far down the hill, followed by most of the troops from the area of the Sandbag Battery. The brigade gets into an impossible position, is fired on from above by fresh troops; Cathcart is killed and his
Another Yakutsk battalion gets into position on Fore Ridge in 'The Gap'; threatening to cut off the Duke of Cambridge's troops at the Sandbag Battery.	

RUSSIAN

ALLIES

force dispersed. Kinglake calls this 'The False Victory'. The Duke of Cambridge, cut off at the Sandbag Battery, narrowly escapes capture.

Assistant Surgeon Wolseley of the 20th, from his aid post established in the Sandbag Battery, leads a charge against the Russians in 'The Gap'.

0830

The French are at last persuaded by Bourbaki to move. The French attack, avoiding the lure of the Sandbag Battery, and reach the base of the Inkerman Tusk.

At the end of the Second Period, the intervention of the French, on the right, had at last stabilized the area of the Sandbag Battery, described as the '*abattoir*' by Bosquet when he saw it. Repeated attacks on Home Ridge during this period had been repelled. The British had, however, lost half of their original strength of 4,700, while Dannenberg still had 9,000 men in reserve, 8,000 men in the fighting line, and 100 guns in battery on Shell Hill.

Third period
0830–0915

RUSSIAN

ALLIES

Dannenberg concentrates his attack on Home Ridge with about 12 battalions (6,000 men). The Russian vanguard advances through the thick

The French 7th *Léger* arrives on Home Ridge.

Egerton with the 77th (from Light Division) arrives near Home Ridge. Pennefather

RUSSIAN

brushwood and captures three British guns on the left of the British line. The Russian vanguard is followed by a massive main 'trunk-column'. The Russians overrun the 55th on the British right, but, coming under fire from their own guns, falter.

The Russian main column overruns the Barrier, while the vanguard reaches the top of Home Ridge.

The main 'trunk-column' reaches Home Ridge, is met, and driven back to the Barrier.

ALLIES

thus awaits the attack with about 3,000 men, Sir George Brown leads a few French troops into a counter-attack and is wounded.

The 7th *Léger* under pressure, withdraws from the line, but rallies in the area of 2nd Division Camp.

In the nick of time Egerton and the 77th come between the Russians and the 2nd Division's camp. The 7th *Léger* takes heart and faces the front. The Russian advance is checked.

The British force at the Barrier withdraws to join the troops on Fore Ridge.

A small force of Zouaves is added to the line on the left of 7th *Léger*.

30 men of the 55th (Daubeney) charge from the British left into the flank of the 'great trunk-column'. The 7th *Léger*, encouraged by this attack, charges head-on into the front of the Russians, backed by Bellairs and Vaughan (retreating from the Barrier). Guns on

ALLIES

Home Ridge pour grape and canister into the Russian masses.

The third period thus ends with the averting of a great crisis. The Russians, attacking with fresh troops, had reached their objective—Home Ridge, only to be driven back by a handful of troops, in an infantry equivalent of the charge of the Heavy Brigade.

Fourth Period
0915–1030

RUSSIAN	ALLIES
The Russian artillery is concentrated on the troops at the Barrier.	The British continue to defend the Barrier; the French are attacked in the area of the Sandbag Battery.
0930	The two 18-pounders ordered earlier by Lord Raglan arrive from the Siege Park, dragged
Timoviev attacks Mount Rodolphe on the French front.	by 150 men under Col Dickson (who later wins VC). They are put into action at Hill Bend, the junction of Fore and Home Ridges, and concentrate their fire on the enemy artillery on Shell Hill.
1000 The enemy artillery fire begins to slacken. Fighting continues at the Barrier.	They are joined by 12 French heavy guns. Bosquet arrives with 2,000 infantry on the right flank.

The long-deferred arrival of the 18-pounders is the turning-point of the battle. Bosquet's arrival secures the difficult right flank, the defence of which absorbed so many troops in unnecessary fighting for the useless Sandbag Battery.

Fifth Period
1000–1100

RUSSIAN	ALLIES
The Russians attack the French on the Inkerman Tusk, drive them out, and reoccupy the Sandbag Battery.	Bosquet, joined by Autemarre's Brigade and the remnants of the Light Brigade, forms up for attack on the right of the Post Road and advances to the Inkerman Tusk.
	They are soon in difficulties, and are forced to withdraw to Fore Ridge. The cavalry remain in reserve, but suffer casualties from artillery fire while waiting under cover.
The Selinghinsk battalions at the Sandbag Battery are routed, and driven back to the Chernaya.	Bosquet, determined to redeem this failure, orders the Zouaves to attack the Sandbag Battery, where they are joined by the Coldstream in a successful attack.

At the end of this period General Canrobert concentrated the French forces in the area from the Kitspur to Home Ridge, and made no further moves against the enemy.

Sixth Period
1100–1300

RUSSIAN	ALLIES
The Russians begin to entrench the ground won on Shell Hill.	Raglan asks for news from Pennefather, who replies that, if reinforced, he is

RUSSIAN

ALLIES

confident of ending the battle. Canrobert, however, cannot be persuaded to act.

The 18-pounders are out of ammunition (having fired 100 rounds each). More is brought up with great difficulty.

Raglan is determined not to let the Russians occupy Shell Hill. While Haines holds the Barrier, Lord West, now commanding the 1st Brigade of 4th Division, orders Acton (77th) to pick up companies of 88th and 21st and attack the West Jut of Shell Hill, supported by the 18-pounders. The attack causes the Russian batteries to limber up and withdraw, and precipitates the Russian retreat.

1300 Dannenberg decides to withdraw; covered by the Vladimir Regiment, his troops are ordered out of the line.

The offensive spirit of the British infantry was never better seen than at this moment. Pennefather, with no more than 750 men left, tired after a long battle, staged an attack against the enemy reserves, on commanding ground, and thus caused the Russian commander to abandon the field.

Last Period
1300–2000

RUSSIAN

ALLIES

1300 The Vladimir battalions advance in mass to cover the

Canrobert declines to join in the pursuit. Todleben

RUSSIAN

retreat, and are broken up by the 18-pounders.

Prince Menshikov orders Dannenberg to halt the retreat.
Dannenberg replies that if he does, the army will be destroyed.
) All enemy artillery withdrawn from Shell Hill. The withdrawal is now covered by fire from steamships in the Roads.

)

Col Todleben forms a flank guard of the Uglitz and Butirsk regiments, and foils Waddy's enterprise.
Russian withdrawal is completed without further incident.

ALLIES

considered this to be a wise decision, and that had tired troops attempted to follow up beyond the range of their heavy guns, they would have come under the guns of the town defences and of the ships, and would have suffered heavy casualties.

General Canrobert occupies the East Jut with two battalions and one battery. In the late afternoon Col Waddy with one company of the 50th from the Victoria Ridge, makes an attempt to cut off Soimonov's artillery retreating in the Careenage Ravine.

Out of their attacking force of some 40,000 the Russians lost 10,729 men at Inkerman, killed, wounded or prisoners, including six generals and 256 officers.

The British lost 597 killed, 1,860 wounded, with 39 officers killed, and 91 wounded.

The French lost 130 killed, 750 wounded, with 13 officers killed, 36 wounded.

On the French left front, General Timoviev attacked at 9.30 am, breaking into the French siege-works on Mount Rodolphe and spiking some guns. His force was counter-attacked in the centre by De Lourmel's brigade, and on the flanks by Levaillant and Aurelle.

Prince Napoleon, with two battalions, was moved west in support.

Timoviev withdrew under the guns of the Quarantine Land Fort, where the French, in pursuit, were cut up by heavy fire. The fighting ended at 11.30 am.

The battle of Inkerman created a stalemate in the Crimea. It ended the allied hope of capturing Sevastopol before the winter; it prevented any further offensive by the Russians, and lastly, it broke the back of the British Army. Officers discovered that their men would not necessarily follow them against the enemy. Many old, faithful, and experienced officers, NCOs and soldiers, were dead or invalided away. Their replacements were never to capture again the spirit which had driven their predecessors up the heights of the Alma, and which had enabled the few to stand against the many in the scrub at Inkerman. In the 'Soldier's Battle' not all had been heroic; in battle the cowards often survive, perhaps eventually to out-number the fearless.

In the Crimea, the scale of warfare and weapons had outrun one vital element in war—communications. The old system of verbal orders, bugles and trumpets, was now insufficient to cope with the manœuvre of masses of troops among the din of musketry and gunfire. The field telephone was not yet invented; the heliograph did not arrive until later. Those who blamed the generals and battalion commanders for lack of directives had probably never tried to control a thousand men in broken country, under fire, with the voice alone. Inkerman was a battle of initiative and opportunity—the uncontrolled British took their chances magnificently—the more cautious and professional French came again dangerously near to failure in the early stages of the battle. However, once Bosquet's troops had been persuaded to attack, their intervention secured the perilous situation on the right flank. The claim that Bosquet was the 'hero of Inkerman' which can be found in pro-French accounts of the battle, do not bear close examination. If there was a hero among the leaders, it was undoubtedly Pennefather.

CHAPTER X

Administrative Difficulties

Administration can be defined as the business of supplying any community with its needs—material and moral. Within the army these needs could at that time be listed as follows:

MATERIAL	Bodily	water, food, clothing, shelter, fire for warmth and cooking.
	Military	arms, ammunition, war stores, spares and tools.
	Transport	animals—forage, shoeing, veterinary service.
		vehicles—repair services, roads, waterborne transport, etc.
	Medical	first aid, hygiene, sanitation, hospitals and convalescent homes, medical stores.
	Financial	pay.
MORAL	Discipline	including police and traffic control.
	Religion	church services, burials.
	Links with home	post, home leave, newspapers.
	Recreation and welfare	games, leave centres, comforts, entertainments.

In the modern army each of these requirements is the particular duty of the various officers and NCOs within the regiment; beyond that it becomes the responsibility of

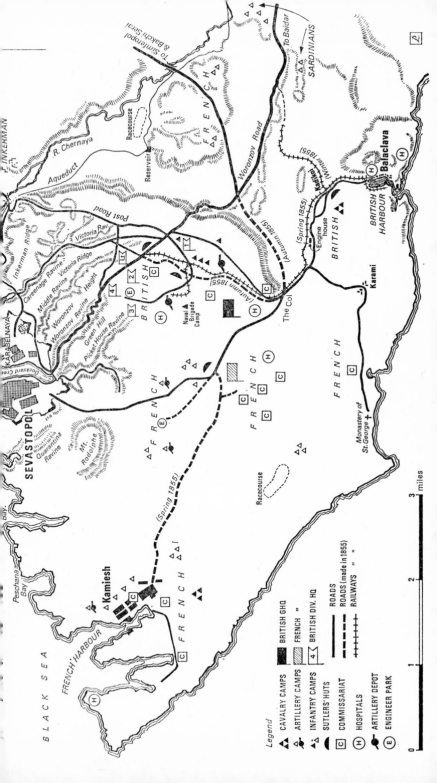

Legend

CAVALRY CAMPS	△△
ARTILLERY CAMPS	△
INFANTRY CAMPS	△∴
SUTLERS' HUTS	▬
COMMISSARIAT	C
HOSPITALS	H
ARTILLERY DEPOT	▲
ENGINEER PARK	E

BRITISH GHQ	■
FRENCH	▨
BRITISH DIV. HQ	4◁
ROADS	—
ROADS (made in 1855)	- - -
RAILWAYS " "	+++

BLACK SEA

Peschana Bay

FRENCH HARBOUR

▲Kamiesh

(Spring 1855)

FRENCH

Racecourse

Monastery of St. George

FRENCH

Karami

BRITISH HARBOUR

Balaclava

BRITISH

The Col

Naval Brigade Camp

Engine house

Kadikoi

(Autumn 1855)

(Spring 1855)

(Autumn 1855)

(Winter 1855)

Woronzov Road

SARDINIANS

To Baidar

To Simferopol & Bakchi Serai

FRENCH

Racecourse

Reservoir

Aqueduct

R. Chernaya

INKERMAN

SEVASTOPOL

KARABELNAYA

Dockyard Creek

Mt. Rodolphe

Quarantine Ravine

Picket House Ravine

Green Hill

Woronzov Ravine

Woronzov Height

Middle Ravine

Carenage Ravine

Victoria Ravine

Victoria Ridge

Inkerman Ridge

Post Road

Victoria Rav.

0 1 2 3 miles

2

the specialist service corps—Transport, Ordnance, Medical, Electrical and Mechanical, Military Police, Catering, Pay, etc., co-ordinated by the staff, divided (in the British Army) into G (General Staff) which deals with operations, A (Adjutant-General's Branch) which deals with personnel, and Q (Quartermaster-General's Branch) which deals with material matters. All this elaborate web of responsibility is linked under the hands of the responsible commanders by a complex and efficient network of communication—nowadays using every modern aid—from the typewriter to the tele-printer, telephone and wireless.

Before the Crimean War, the Army was administered by the following staff of officials:

(1) The Secretary of State for War and the Colonies, in theory responsible for military policy, but largely occupied by Colonial Office business (in which building he worked).

(2) The Secretary-at-War, at the Horse Guards, dealing with army business and finance in Parliament.

(3) The Commander-in-Chief, at the Horse Guards, the supreme commander. He could initiate no measure involving finance, without the agreement of the Secretary-at-War.

(4) The Adjutant-General, who dealt with recruiting, dis-cipline, pay, arms, clothing and necessaries.

(5) The Quartermaster-General, who dealt with movement, quartering, barracks, camps, and transport (though no transport corps existed).

(6) The Board of General Officers who advised the Adjutant-General on clothing and equipment.

(7) The Master-General of the Ordnance who commanded and trained the artillery and engineers and headed the Board of Ordnance.

(8) Commanding officers of regiments who dealt with contractors for rations and fuel.

(9) Abroad, the Commissariat officers (who held military rank) provided rations and fuel and managed butcheries and bakeries. They were responsible direct to the Treasury.

(10) The Medical Staff Corps of doctors, and purveyors (quartermasters to hospitals) worked partly under the Secretary-at-War, the Commander-in-Chief and the Ordnance office.

(11) The Paymaster-General had an independent office, and acted as cashier for the Treasury to the Army. Regimental paymasters drew and disbursed pay to the men, and kept the muster rolls of the regiment, rendering their accounts direct to the Secretary-at-War. The Army Pay Department (1877) became the Army Pay Corps in 1893.

None of these offices was co-ordinated; their duties were ill-defined; communication was only by letter. There was no effort at training for war, nor to adapt the system to changing times.

In the Crimea, the specialist administrative corps were as follows:

The Board of Ordnance was the oldest administrative body in the Army, having been in existence since the Middle Ages. By the nineteenth century it was responsible for providing the artillery and engineers with their equipment, and for clothing and supplying the whole army with arms, ammunition, and accommodation. There was, however, no co-ordinated store-keeping department for dealing with the huge variety of items, and it was not until the appointment of a half-pay officer, Capt Gordon, as Ordnance Storekeeper in the Crimea in September, 1855, that the departments of Ordnance were consolidated; the Quartermaster-General's stores, the engineering departments, the siege train stores, the Purveyor's stores and the stocks of the Army Work Corps, Army Transport Train, and the railway were all centralized under one department.

In London, the Board of Ordnance had no head, having been robbed of its Master-General (Lord Raglan) and of the Surveyor-General, who also went to the war.

The present-day Royal Army Ordnance Corps, which grew out of the old organizations, was formed in 1865.

The Royal Wagon Train, an embryo transport corps founded in 1794 in Flanders, had been disbanded in 1833 and its wagons sold at auction. Mr Filder, the Commissary, who had learnt his business with the Duke, tried, at Varna, to get his Commissariat Transport working—but his pack animals were left behind, and he was forced to operate in the Crimea with 80 horses and mules, a few Maltese carts, and 80 native carts captured from the Russians.

In March, 1855, a Land Transport Corps was formed, under Col McMurdo; by the end of the campaign it reached a strength of 9,000 all ranks with 24,000 animals. Renamed the Military Train after the war, it eventually became the Royal Army Service Corps in 1870, and is now the Royal Corps of Transport.

The Army Medical Services were still non-existent. Regiments made their own medical arrangements; surgeons, apothecaries and dispensers were commissioned into regiments. In May, 1854, a Hospital Conveyance Corps was formed, manned by unemployed pensioners, and designed for the carriage of sick and wounded. In August, 1856, this corps was incorporated into the Land Transport Corps.

In June, 1855, a new Medical Staff Corps was founded, to provide hospital services. It was composed of nine companies, each responsible for a 500-bed hospital. A company had one section working under the Purveyor (stewards, ration issuers, washermen and cooks), and one section under the Surgeon (wardmasters, barbers, and nursing orderlies), a strength in all of 120.

After the war, in 1857, the Medical Staff Corps was reorganized as the Army Hospital Corps, changing in 1898 to the Royal Army Medical Corps of today.

Veterinary officers had been appointed to the cavalry and artillery since 1796—they were gazetted to regiments and worked within the regiment, equipped with two regimental and two troop veterinary chests of medicines.

In the Peninsula 'sick-horse depots' had been formed, but this practice had been forgotten, and there were no veterinary hospitals in the Crimea. The regimental system was abolished after 1870, when all 'vets' were appointed to the Army Veterinary Department, which became a Royal Corps in 1918.

The attitude in 1854 towards administration as a whole, and towards the common soldier as a human being, was quite different from modern thinking. Many officers regarded their soldiers as little better than brutes, who would be spoilt by being pampered by even the most elementary comforts; many others were simply thoughtless and selfish, caring only for their own comfort, and being quite willing to leave the theatre of war rather than face the hardships of winter. In all regiments there were some who genuinely cared for their men, and did what they could to improve their lot—but these were in a minority.

At any level the administrator must deal not only with the 'logistics' of battle—the movement of vast numbers of men, ammunition, guns and stores against the enemy—but also with the struggle against the elements—heat, cold, thirst, hunger, disease, exposure, and the more insidious factors of boredom, battle-fatigue, dissidence, and loss of morale.

These facts are (or should be) commonplace to every Sandhurst cadet today, but it is safe to say that there were few in the Crimea who could either view the problem as a whole, or who had the power of organization to deal with it. The British system in those days was to fight the war first and let the administration take care of itself. The French knew better; their Services, founded under Napoleon, were a model to the rest of Europe.

Details of the administrative services of the French Army of the Crimea can be found in the first volume of Bazancourt's *Expedition de la Crimée*. Their General Staff was far more comprehensive than the British equivalent, including officers of all arms, of the *Intendance* (the administrative service) and of special political and geographical departments, treasury, postal, and military police.

The *Intendance* included a comprehensive medical and hospital service, transport, victualling, clothing, and accommodation services, veterinary, provost and chaplain's departments. All were represented at divisional level.

At Kamiesh the French built a hutted town, of some 100 acres in extent, for their Commissariat Department and a further 50 acres of shops in which a large variety of goods could be bought.

In the line the French adopted the now obvious course of putting formations into the trenches complete with their own chain of command and administrative services. Examination of the British system at the siege of Sevastopol reveals a serious fault, in that men were put haphazardly into the trenches with one officer to 50 men, with no clearly defined chain of command, and often no co-ordinating commander whatever.

It was this lack of a working chain of command, with a clear allotment of responsibility, which lay behind all the British Army's difficulties in the Crimea, and which made it so hard for the knots of the administrative tangle to be cut.

Other British administrative defects had been shown up early in the campaign; the troops had landed without many essentials; their load, 63 lb per man, was cumbersome and badly attached, with the result that many awkward items, such as the camp-kettle, essential for cooking, were discarded. Much of the equipment, left over from the Peninsula, was rotten; billhooks and entrenching tools broke in the hand, canvas and leather were decayed; coats and boots fell to pieces.

Once in position before Sevastopol, the French, already better equipped, had an easier haul from the spacious harbour at Kamiesh to their camps; the British, at Balaclava, were not only much further from their harbour, which was cramped and inadequate, but were also faced with the climb of 600 feet from sea-level to the Sapouné Heights up the winding, and unmetalled track to The Col—three miles, and then three more to the divisional camps, and two more to the front line.

To keep an army in the field, in front of Sevastopol, in winter, efficiently and well supplied, would tax a more modern military machine; it would certainly require five or six men behind the line to every one in it.

Lord Raglan had not the men, and he and his staff lacked the ability to organize. There was no one with the drive and skill of Todleben or Kornilov, who by example, energy, and improvisation, achieved the miracle of organizing the defence of Sevastopol. The British needed a dynamo, who could ride here and there, cursing, threatening, cajoling, insisting, and above all sorting out the priorities. It was not that stores and food were not there at Balaclava; they were there in plenty, as all contemporary accounts show. The harbour was full of 'rotten wood, rotten hay, rotten meal and cargo of every description'. Baled hay was even used for landing stages.

The most successful British unit administratively was undoubtedly the Naval Brigade. Formed on 1 October, 1854, this force, composed of officers and sailors from the fleet, was responsible for manning about 35 guns in the siege batteries. Their camp was better constructed, their sanitary arrangements more efficient, and their independent transport system ensured a steady supply of food, with the result that their casualties from sickness were the lowest in the Army. Field-Marshal Sir Evelyn Wood was at that time a midshipman serving with the Naval Brigade; his book *The Crimea in 1854 and 1894* is one of the clearest and most interesting of the eye-witness accounts of the campaign. (Sir Evelyn transferred to the 17th Lancers after the war.) One passage in this book—on the subject of command, is especially cogent: 'In our siege works there were four co-equal and independent forces. The Engineers planned and laid out batteries and parallels; Infantry soldiers found the labour for the works and defended them; Artillerymen and Sailors "mounted" and fought the guns. *Nevertheless for months there was no chief controlling Commander, and thus in the trenches we constantly played at cross purposes.*'

The whole administrative problem was a tragic 'vicious

circle'. With such large distances involved, a good road should have been the first priority, but there was none; even the Woronzov Road was an incomplete link. The Col should have been improved while the good weather lasted. Roads need labour; British labour could not be spared, but 11,000 Turks, who had proved to be inadequate in the line, sat in their camps unused. At one time 400 Turks were employed to try and improve the road, but the work was abandoned at Raglan's orders, when they made little impression on the hard clay soil.

Horses were available for transport, but they were sited up on the plateau, where they starved, while such hay and corn as there was rotted in the harbour. Lord Raglan did order the cavalry to supply 500 horses for transport, but the attempt was badly organized, many horses dying at the work for which they were no longer fit. By mid-January the attempt was abandoned.

Without a road or wheeled transport it was immaterial what arrived at Balaclava. Until the construction of a railway in January, 1855, by navvies brought from England, it was simply impossible to get enough stores uphill.

On the railway, trucks were at first drawn by horses on level ground, and by stationary engines on the steeper gradients. At least five locomotives were later shipped to the Crimea, the names of three, *Alliance*, *Victory* and *Swan*, have been recorded. Railway enthusiasts will find further details in an article by Michael Robbins on the *Balaclava Railway*, Journal of Transport History, 1953.

On this administrative chaos broke the worst winter in living memory. On 14 November a hurricane swept the Crimea, sinking 16 ships, some loaded with stores, including all the warm clothing for the troops. The whole administrative machine broke down; administration became a matter of 'every man for himself'; fighting the enemy gave way to fighting for life against the weather. It was a battle in which too many were on the losing side.

It is almost impossible to visualize nowadays the horror

of the winter of 1854. At the front the soldier, sleeping in wet trenches, with no dry clothes and no floor to his tent when out of the front line, was fed on tiny rations of uncooked food, accompanied by coffee made with green beans, which could not be roasted. With no firewood to warm himself or his food, with his clothes worn out, he became an easy victim to dysentery, scurvy or cholera. A bumpy ride strapped to a mule, or in an unsprung cart or litter, took him to Balaclava harbour, where in an overcrowded ship, he lay on the deck or in the darkness of the hold, while outside the harbour stank with dead animals, amputated limbs, rotting vegetables and the corpses of cholera victims. If he then survived a week's voyage to Scutari, he was brought ashore roughly by Turkish labourers, and finally dumped on the filthy floor of the Barrack Hospital. Here there were no beds, no furniture, no eating utensils, no medical supplies and no blankets. The latrines were clogged and the tubs standing in the passage were never emptied. Men lay naked on the floor in their own excrement. The few doctors were totally overwhelmed; in January and February, 1855, the hospital held 2,350 patients at any one time, and in that period 2,315 men died.

Into this chaos on 5 November, 1854, came Florence Nightingale with 38 nurses. At first the doctors refused to accept her help and her nurses were only allowed to do menial duties, until suddenly the stream of wounded from Balaclava and Inkerman overwhelmed the hospital. Gradually, Florence Nightingale's influence spread; she had £30,000 in her control which she was prepared to dispense on her own initiative; not only did she buy many of the necessities herself, but she worked unceasingly, often without any sleep for days, at organizing the washing of linen, issue of clothing and beds for the patients, cooking special diets, and a thousand other tasks. Under her management the hospital death rate fell from 44 per cent to 2·2 per cent six months later.

The traditional picture of her as the 'Lady with the Lamp', soothing the wounded, is a true one, but it represents the least part of what she did. She tackled a volume of sheer physical hard work, and a quantity of correspondence, which would dismay a staff of twenty trained officers. Her work at Scutari is the very finest example of what one person with determination can achieve, in circumstances which seem hopeless.

She made two visits to the Crimea. On the first, early in May, 1855, she took with her Alexis Soyer, chef of the Reform Club, and another French chef. Soyer had come out to advise on cooking and diet in the Army. After visiting the front and the hospitals she fell ill with cholera and was taken to the Castle Hospital at Balaclava, where she nearly died. She returned to Scutari, narrowly avoiding an underhand effort by Dr John Hall, the chief Medical Officer at the Castle Hospital, to ship her direct to England.

In March, 1856, she was invited to visit the Land Transport Corps Hospital in Balaclava. She arrived with a party of ten nurses, and ran into endless difficulties with Mother Bridgeman who was in charge of the hospital, and with her *bête noire*, now *Sir* John Hall, and Fitzgerald, the Purveyor-in-Chief. She took over the General Hospital, and remained until June, when she returned to Scutari, where she stayed until July when the last man left the Barrack Hospital.

Florence Nightingale died in 1910, having been an invalid since 1857. The whole of the rest of her life was devoted to continuing the work she started in the Crimea— pouring out a ceaseless flow of recommendations and designs on hospital construction, administration, and reform, all over the world. The Army owes her a colossal debt.

The impetus to cut the administrative tangle came also through the Press—not only from the dispatches of *The Times* correspondent W. H. Russell, but from letters in the home papers, from serving officers and their relations at home. Russell was described by Henry Clifford as 'A vulgar low Irishman . . . has a good gift of the gab, and uses his pen as well as his tongue, sings a good song, drinks anyone's brandy-and-water, and smokes as many cigars as foolish young officers will let him . . . he is just the sort to get information, especially out of youngsters.'

Russell and his editor, Delane, hated Lord Raglan, and attacked him unmercifully. Russell had been *chasséd* (Clifford's word) out of Army Headquarters by Raglan, for publishing information useful to the enemy. He and his editor declined to accept guidance on any form of security. *The Times* continually published details of allied strengths, armaments, casualties and state of morale, without the slightest compunction. 'We have no need of spies,' said a Russian general, 'we have *The Times.*'

However, public opinion was stirred up at home, resulting in the fall of Lord Aberdeen's government on 31 January, 1855. Lord Palmerston headed the new administration, in which Lord Panmure was Minister of War and Lord Clarendon Foreign Secretary. Panmure's first move was to send out General Simpson as Chief-of-Staff to Lord Raglan, to help relieve the latter of the load of detail with which he was burdened.

Various charitable funds had been opened in October, 1854. Early in January a steamer left London loaded with £20,000 worth of comforts, ranging from whisky and port to tools, books, wigs and even a street potato-baking machine. The sorting, acknowledgement and distribution of these presents, not always wisely selected, was generally left to Florence Nightingale, who found the task a great additional burden.

As spring approached, the administrative chaos was gradually cleared. A system for the supply of provisions to central depots on the plateau was established; Turkish labour was recruited for construction work; the railway, from Balaclava to the area of the Telegraph on the Woronzov Road, was completed; transport was borrowed from the French; Spanish mules arrived from Barcelona.

Mr Filder, the Commissary-General, began to restore order in Balaclava with the help of Admiral Boxer, appointed to organize the port. Greatcoats and boots began to arrive;

the crowd of dishonest sutlers and contractors, who had been operating unchecked in Balaclava, was brought under control. Huts became available, but as it took two artillery wagons with ten horses, or 180 men, to move a single hut up to the heights, progress was slow. Fresh meat and oranges arrived from Malta; by February the army was on the mend. By March race-meetings were being organized, football and cricket were being played in the camps. It was time to turn against the enemy once more.

At this time the French command was strengthened by the arrival of the formidable General Pélissier. Canrobert formed two Corps, the composition of which was as follows:

```
1st Corps—Pélissier—1st Division—Forey
                  —2nd      ,,      —Levaillant
                  —3rd      ,,      —Pâté
                  —4th      ,,      —De Salles

2nd Corps—Bosquet—1st Division—Bouat
                  —2nd      ,,      —Camon
                  —3rd      ,,      —Mayran
                  —4th      ,,      —Dulac
```

The French now had eight strong divisions, to the depleted British six. For the rest of the war, the French were to be the dominant partner. Less welcome to General Canrobert had been the arrival in January of General Niel, Napoleon's personal representative, who came to keep a check on Canrobert's decisions, and to prepare for the time when the Emperor himself would arrive to take command of the armies.

The British force was so depleted by sickness, that in addition to the Turkish, and, later Sardinian, contingents, the following mercenary troops were recruited—a Polish legion of 1,500 men, a Swiss legion of 3,000 men, and a German legion of about 9,000 men. Part of this last force was sent after the war to the military settlement at the Cape of Good Hope, where many of the officers and men remained after their discharge.

The British were forced to give up the whole of the right flank of the siege to the French, retaining only the two 'attacks' astride the Woronzov Ravine facing the Redan and the head of the Dockyard Creek. The French became responsible for the attack on the Malakov, and for the protection of the northern and eastern flanks of the Inkerman Heights. (See Map 117.)

CHAPTER XI

The Siege of Sevastopol

The course of the campaign was now decided; the Russian army had proved unable to beat the allies in the field. The superior fire-power of the Minié, wielded by the thin lines of the British, had defeated the clumsy slow-moving masses of the Russian infantry, however overwhelming their numbers might seem to be. The Russian cavalry had been ineffective against both cavalry and infantry. The Russian field artillery, however, had proved to be better than either the French or the British; only the timely arrival of the two British 18-pounders at Inkerman had prevented disaster.

The allies, confined to Balaclava and the Upland by superior numbers, had no alternative but to continue in their attempt to take Sevastopol by siege.

Many people visualize the defences of Sevastopol as a continuous stone wall in the style of a medieval walled town. In fact, except for the round tower of the Malakov and another in the Old Town, there was very little stone in the original defences of the town, other than what Sir George Cathcart described as a 'low park wall'.

Todleben's defences consisted entirely of earthworks, reinforced with timber, brushwood, and the cylindrical wattle baskets known as 'gabions'. Gun embrasures were protected by rope mantlets woven by the Russian sailors.

The outline of the basic defence work was as shown in the diagram on page 118.

The rampart was made of earth dug from the ditch, after marking out along the line of the *berme*, a narrow path to facilitate repairs to the face of the work; the *épaulement* was about 15 feet high, with the *banquette* or firestep of sufficient

HE ALLIED POSITIONS
EFORE SEVASTOPOL

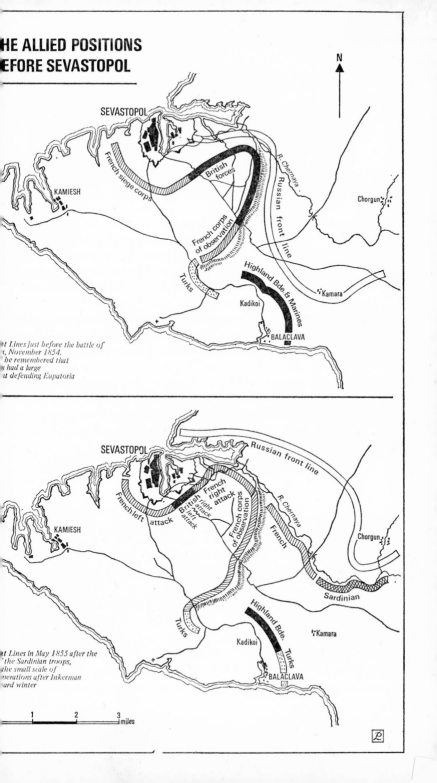

N

SEVASTOPOL

KAMIESH

French siege corps

British forces

R. Chernaya

Russian front line

Chorgun

French corps of observation

Turks

Highland Bde. & Marines

Kamara

Kadikoi

BALACLAVA

*t Lines just before the battle of
*, November 1854.
* be remembered that
*s had a large
t defending Eupatoria

SEVASTOPOL

KAMIESH

Russian front line

French left attack

British right attack

French right attack

British left attack

French corps of observation

R. Chernaya

French

Chorgun

Sardinian

Turks

Highland Bde.

Turks

Kamara

Kadikoi

BALACLAVA

*t Lines in May 1855 after the
* the Sardinian troops,
* the small scale of
*perations after Inkerman
ard winter

| 1 | 2 | 3 miles |

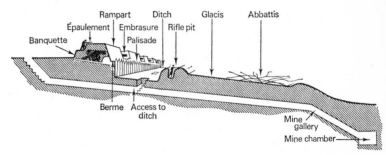

height to enable the defending infantry to fire over the top when attacked. The palisade was of sharpened stakes, while the *abbattis* on the *glacis* consisted of a tangle of trees designed to impede the attacker—it was generally about 100 yards in front of the ditch. The ground was also littered with planks studded with sharp nails.

Fougasses, holes filled with stones, with a detonating charge which flung them upwards, were sited on the forward slopes and were sometimes fired electrically. Both sides carried on a continual mine-warfare, especially on the French left front, facing the Flagstaff Bastion, where the earth was suitable for this type of operation.

Guns in embrasures had little lateral traverse, so on occasions they were mounted '*en barbette*' that is high enough to fire over the top of the rampart.

The common shapes of defence work were as follows:

In continuous works the *gorge* or entrance to the back of the work was left open, and covered by the fire of a further line of defence sited behind. Thus an attacker who entered the work would find himself immediately under heavy fire from the reserve positions, from which a counter-attack would soon be launched.

Examination of the plan on page 120 will show the scale

of these works; it must be realized that the Malakov was 250 yards in depth, backed by an elaborate system of reserve works, and shelter pits for the infantry assembled for counter-attack.

At Sevastopol, Todleben had the advantage of superior supplies of stone and timber from buildings in the town, of materials from the dockyard, and of guns and ammunition from the ships. The Russian capacity for digging was also greater than that of either of the allied armies, especially when the latter became weakened by exposure and lack of food. Brushwood became unobtainable on the upland plateau.

The making of *gabions* was a very laborious task. Sir Evelyn Wood says that in the Guards Brigade, a section of three men could make three each day, but in the Line regiments only one—a comment on the difference in efficiency of the officers. British soldiers were paid 14*d* for each *gabion* passed as serviceable, and 7*d* for a *fascine*, a long thin faggot lying horizontally on the face of the earthwork; the task included the cutting and carriage of the brushwood.

In the battle of wits and hard work, which is the pattern of a siege, the Russians, guided by the genius of Todleben, had completely mastered the situation. The allies used the well-tried method of establishing parallels, linked by zig-zag saps, to bring the assaulting troops and batteries nearer to the defence. But to every move made by the allies, Todleben had an answer; overnight a new Russian work would appear to counter any allied threat. The Russian works were screened by rifle-pits, from which aggressive sorties were made against the allied works. French and British responded by trying the same system to protect their trenches; then the Russian sailors arrived with boat-hooks and ropes to drag the French riflemen out of their holes. Canrobert wrote in protest to Menshikov against this undignified method of warfare, which was courteously discontinued. The British, being short-handed, and with their ranks filled by inexperienced reinforcements, were particularly vulnerable to surprise attack by patrols.

9

Copy of the original Royal Engineers' survey—Sevastopol Section.
Scale about 600 yards to the inch. British parallels are marked
RIGHT ATTACK and LEFT ATTACK. At this period, September 1855,
the French occupied all the rest of the works. Note how close they
are to the Malakov and the Little Redan. Note also the bridges of

boats in the harbour and the Dockyard Creek; the importance of the
Mamelon, now in French hands; the distance of the British right
attack from the Redan, and the tactical ineffectiveness of the British
left attack, except as a fire-base.

On 10 January the Russians made a feint attack on Balaclava from the direction of Kamara. This move was designed to divert attention from the fact that Liprandi's army was about to be moved northwards to join General Osten-Sacken in an attack on Eupatoria, which was defended by a force of about 30,000 Turks under General Omar Pasha. The Turks at Eupatoria were stiffened by French and British officers, and by sailors and marines from both fleets. Liprandi and Osten-Sacken had about 36 battalions, 80 guns, and six regiments of cavalry under command. The defences consisted of a simple semi-circular earthwork on the land side, mounting about 100 guns; at the left end it was guarded by five French ships grounded, but with their guns still in action, while three British warships, one French and one Turkish steamer were in general support.

The Russians attacked on 17 January, with heavy artillery fire all along the line, including some 32-pounders. The greatest pressure was exerted against the Turkish right, where an assault with ladders was tried. Three attempts were all broken up by artillery fire, by a rocket party from the British ship *Viper* and by the Turkish cavalry. The Russians finally withdrew, with some 2,500 casualties against 350 from the garrison.

Omar Pasha further strengthened the defences of Eupatoria, while the Turkish cavalry continued to operate actively in the plain, keeping the Russians at a safe distance from the town.

Back at Balaclava the absence of Liprandi's army had been detected. It was planned on the night of 20 February for Sir Colin Campbell, with 2,000 of his own brigade, and 4,000 French, under Bosquet, to cross the Chernaya at night, and to capture the holding party left behind in Liprandi's camp.

The plan was frustrated by a violent blizzard. The troops ploughed about all night in blinding snow, unable to find their way, and were forced to keep marching in circles to avoid frost-bite.

Two nights later the Russians made a move which was

to have a great influence on the siege. About 400 yards in front of the Malakov, facing the French (who had now taken over this sector of the Victoria Ridge), was a small hill called the Mamelon Vert. On the night of 22 February the Russians rapidly converted the Mamelon into a redoubt faced with stone. Bosquet recognized its importance at once; the Mamelon was attacked and captured, but it could not be held. After four nights fighting the Russians were still in possession, having further strengthened the fortifications by the installation of ten 24-pounders.

On 2 March, Czar Nicholas died, and was succeeded by his son Alexander II, who decided to continue the war. Menshikov was replaced in command of the Russian army by Gorchakov.

The Russians opened new entrenchments, known as the White Works, to the north of the French positions overlooking the Careenage Ravine; on 23 March, they made a determined sortie from the Mamelon against the French parallels on the Victoria Ridge. After establishing themselves in the French lines, they turned against the north flank of the British right attack, but were driven out before reaching the batteries.

On 9 April, the allies opened the Second Bombardment of Sevastopol. The numbers of guns were as follows: British 138, French 362, Russian 998. The bombardment was continued for nearly a fortnight. The Russians were short of men, since they had just dispatched a force for another attack on Eupatoria, having observed the departure of Omar Pasha and a large Turkish detachment for the Chersonese. The Russian force was hastily recalled, when the allied bombardment began.

The railway was now working well—by the end of April it was handling 240 tons of ammunition and stores per day.

Lord Raglan pressed for an assault to follow the bombardment. Canrobert resisted steadily, tied down by instructions from Napoleon III, who now had ideas of himself commanding an army in the field, elsewhere in the Crimea. Further confusion was added by the Conference of Vienna, which had opened on 15 March, attended by Austria, France, Great Britain, Russia and Turkey, to discuss the possibility of peace. Russia, however, had little intention of accepting the terms suggested. As long as Todleben continued to repair the damage done by the allied guns, there was no need to yield to the allied demands, so the April attack petered out indecisively.

Pélissier, however, was beginning to make himself felt. Early in May, against Canrobert's wishes, he insisted on attacking the Russian outworks guarding the Central Bastion. The attack was successful, and the new spirit of aggression on the French side was most heartening to the British.

At this time the electric telegraph from Varna was completed to British and French Headquarters. This fact, which should have been a benefit to the allies, proved to be the opposite, for it brought Napoleon III close enough to his commander-in-chief to hamper him greatly.

A combined expedition to Kertch, at the entrance to the Sea of Azov, sailed on 2 May. This venture, of British conception, was designed to cut off the Russian supplies coming from that area, and to open the Sea of Azov to allied gunboats, which could then operate against Russian coastal traffic bringing supplies from the mainland. The force consisted of 8,000 French under Forey, 4,000 British under Sir George Brown, and 3,000 Turks.

Two hours after the expedition had sailed Canrobert received a telegram from Napoleon III ordering him to concentrate all his forces to 'attack the enemy externally'. To Raglan's despair, Canrobert insisted on recalling the expedition.

The Emperor's plan followed: one army to remain in the siege of Sevastopol; one to attack the Mackenzie Heights from Balaclava; one to make a diversion either further east in the valley of Baidar against Alushta, or from Eupatoria against Simferopol.

Canrobert, feeling his position to be impossible, resigned his command to Pélissier on 19 May. Pélissier's corps was taken by de Salles, while Canrobert took command of a division.

On 8 May the Sardinian army under General Marmora arrived in Balaclava, that country having joined the Allies on 26 January. The Sardinians were put into position on the Balaclava front, where the allies now held the line of the Chernaya. Two fresh British cavalry regiments, the 10th Hussars and 12th Lancers, were now patrolling in this area.

On 22 May the expedition to Kertch sailed for the second time, Pélissier boldly defying his Emperor's orders, in giving his consent to the operation. The expedition was very successful; without loss, Kertch and Yenikale were taken, 100 guns captured, thousands of tons of corn and flour were destroyed, Russian steamers sunk, factories destroyed, and arsenals and magazines blown up. The Sea of Azov was opened to British gun-boats, which entered and did enormous damage to the Russian supplies. A French garrison was left in the town.

Before Sevastopol, the French continued their struggle to capture the Russian outworks in front of the Central Bastion and the Flagstaff Battery.

On 6 June, the Third Bombardment of Sevastopol was begun. The object was for the French to capture the Mamelon and the White Works, which enfiladed the ground in front of the Malakov, while the British attacked the Quarries, which guarded the approaches to the Redan. The guns employed were as follows: British 159, French 436, Russian, 1,174.

By 9 June, all three attacks had succeeded, in spite of desperate Russian counter-attacks; confidence returned, and the capture of the Malakov and the Redan now seemed to be within sight.

The assault on the main works followed ten days later. After a heavy bombardment (the Fourth *) on 17 June, the

*Guns—British 166, French 429, Russian 1,129.

French attacked the Malakov, and the British the Redan; the result was a disastrous failure on both fronts.

The Russians were ready—it was the anniversary of Waterloo—and allied deserters had taken news of the attack to the enemy.

On the British front, the artillery fire stopped at the critical moment; the enemy's barrage of grape and musketry was the heaviest Raglan had ever seen. The British had 450 yards of ground to cross, under this devastating fire. The attack withered and died, as the officers went down and the men refused to follow.

On the French front, Pélissier had altered the zero hour from 1.30 am to 3.30 am (dawn) when a bouquet of fireworks would signal the attack. At 2.50 General Mayran mistook three shells from the Mamelon for the signal; his division attacked prematurely, and was cut to pieces before reaching the Malakov. Autemarre's troops captured the Gervais battery, to the left of the Malakov, but were driven out by the Russians waiting behind. The principle of defence of the Russian redoubts—that of leaving the 'gorge' at the back open—was highly successful. Pélissier withdrew the French forces, and by 8.30 am the battle was over.

The British lost 1,500 men; Sir John Campbell and Lacy Yea were among those killed; the French lost 1,600 wounded and 1,500 killed, including Generals Brunet and Mayran.

The disappointment was intense; the successes of 9 June had aroused everyone's hopes. At Headquarters there was an air of despair; cholera and fever struck at men of lowered resistance; on 24 June, Estcourt, the Adjutant-General, died and four days later Lord Raglan succumbed as well. On 3 July, his body was carried in state to the *Caradoc*, in Kazach Bay, to be conveyed to England.

On 20 June, Todleben was wounded and took no further part in the campaign. He had, however, a long military future in front of him; in the Russo-Turkish War of 1877, he was in command of siege works against the Bulgarian fortresses; after that war he became Commander-in-Chief of the whole Russian army; he died in 1884, aged 66.

At the time of Raglan's death Sir George Brown, the next senior officer, was already under medical orders to return home; Sir James Simpson was confirmed in command of the army on 1 July. The British order of battle at this period is given in Appendix V.

On 16 August, Gorchakov launched an attack with four infantry divisions and two artillery brigades, across the Chernaya, to recapture the Fediukine Heights, as a base for further operations against Balaclava and the Sapouné Heights.

The Chernaya was held by the French, with a bridge-head in the centre, over the Traktir Bridge, with the Sardinians on their right, opposite Chorgun, supported by a British 32-pounder battery. The Turks under Osman Pasha occupied the Marine Heights; the British and French cavalry covered the entrance to the valley of Baidar (which lay beyond Kamara on the Woronzov Road).

The Russians, after diversionary movements in the valley of Baidar, descended from the Mackenzie Heights under cover of darkness. The right column, facing the French, was commanded by General Read (an officer of Scots descent) and the left by Liprandi. The Russian 7th Division, in their left column, made first contact with the Sardinians, who were driven back to the river. On the extreme left of the French line, the Russian 5th Division crossed the river, but was stopped by the French on the line of the aqueduct.

In the centre, General Read led the massed attack of the Russian 12th Division on Traktir Bridge. The attack succeeded in driving back the French, but the Russian advance on to the slopes of the Fediukine hills was met by a determined counter-attack with the bayonet. The Russians now threw in their reserve division, the 17th, on the French right.

Six batteries of French horse artillery, held in reserve, were brought smartly into action opposite this new threat, while Pélissier brought up from his reserves, Levaillant's division, Dulac's division and the Imperial Guard.

The Russians were trying to split the French and the Sardinians, but General Marmora filled in the danger-point by aligning his Piedmontese Division along the aqueduct, supported by Sardinian and British cavalry in reserve. A last effort by an Odessa battalion was stopped, with heavy loss, at the aqueduct. The Russians turned and left the battlefield. No cavalry pursuit was attempted; once across the Chernaya, any pursuer would have come under the Russian guns, impregnably sited on the Mackenzie Heights.

The French lost about 300 killed or missing, and 1,200 wounded; the Russians, more than 3,000 killed, and perhaps 7,000 wounded; General Read was killed.

The Russians had learnt little from Inkerman; their massed columns were still thrown brutally against the allied rifles, with the same results. The French and Sardinians were well handled at all levels; except for Mowbray's 32-pounders, the British took no part. The Turks, under Osman Pasha, remained firmly in their defensive positions.

The Battle of the Chernaya is usually ignored in British history books. It was important in that it represented the Russians' last effort to break the Allied siege by operations in the field. Immediately after their defeat, the Russians began to lay a bridge of boats across Sevastopol harbour to the North Side, an indication that their confidence in holding the city was ebbing.

Rumours of another attack in the Chernaya area persuaded General Simpson to secure Balaclava by moving the Highland Division to the area of the Kamara Heights, while the French constructed three new redoubts covering the Traktir Bridge. The railway was extended through Kadikoi, towards Chorgun, and the whole eastern flank was thoroughly strengthened.

The Allies had opened the Fifth Bombardment* of Sevastopol on 17 August, during the Chernaya battle; a week of alarms and cannonading followed. What was hoped to be the final assault was planned for 5 September.

*Guns employed: British 182, French 522, Russian 1,209.

It had become clear, in the course of the siege, that the Malakov was the key to Sevastopol. Without silencing the Malakov, the Redan could not be taken; without taking the Redan, the ground behind the Flagstaff Bastion was useless to an attacker. It was necessary to stake all upon the capture of the Malakov. A diversion against the Redan would have been sufficient to allow the French to take the Malakov; but unfortunately the Redan was now the only possible objective on the British front and national pride dictated that the British must attack the Redan, if the French attacked the Malakov.

The plan was for a three-day bombardment (the Sixth)* starting on 5 September, with an attack on the 8th, the French against the Little Redan, the Malakov, and the Curtain joining the two; the British against the Redan. The bombardment was the heaviest in history; the French fired rapidly, the British slowly and deliberately, reserving their main effort for the last day.

The British attack was to be led by 100 men of the Rifle Brigade, followed by 100 snipers from the Buffs, to pick off the enemy gunners, and 320 men of the Light Division carrying 40 scaling ladders, 24 feet long. Codrington was to command the assault, with the remaining British troops in support and reserve. General Simpson took his post in the second parallel.

On the French left, commanded by de Salles, attacks were to be made on the Central Bastion (Levaillant), and on the Flagstaff Bastion (Autemarre) with a Sardinian brigade in reserve.

On the French right—Bosquet's Inkerman Attack—the Malakov was to be stormed by MacMahon's division; the Little Redan by Dulac's division supported by the Imperial Guard, and a brigade from Aurelle's division. The Curtain was to be attacked by the division of La Motte Rouge. Each corps was to be accompanied by 60 sappers, 300 men with scaling ladders, and 50 artillerymen detailed either to

*Guns employed: British 183, French 592, Russian 1,209.

spike the Russian guns, or to turn them against the enemy.

At 8 am on the morning of 8 September, three French mines, each of 3,000 lb of powder, were exploded in front of the Malakov. At 10 am Pélissier took post in the Mamelon to watch the attack.

Gorchakov, on the Inkerman Heights, watched the preparations, but believed that Pélissier was still awaiting a consignment of 200 mortars from France, before undertaking the capture of the city. Zero hour was to be at midday—without signals; the disaster of the previous assault had been aggravated by the mistaken signal to attack. Watches had been carefully synchronized; the French left attack, and the British attack on the Redan were, however, not to begin until the French flag was hoisted on the Malakov.

Noon was chosen as the hour at which the enemy would be least likely to expect attack; it was not only the hour for the midday meal, but the time at which the Russians changed their pickets.

The French right attack was very successful, the parallels having been driven to within 25 yards of the Malakov. The leading troops of MacMahon's division sprang up and were into the fort without a shot fired. The Russians were completely surprised, and in spite of desperate attempts to counter-attack, never regained their hold on the Malakov.

On the right, the division La Motte Rouge pierced the Curtain, spiking a six-gun battery covering the Malakov, but at the Little Redan, Dulac's division was driven out with heavy losses. Pélissier ordered that no further attempts were to be made on that flank, but that all efforts were to be concentrated on retaining the Malakov.

On the French left, the attack on the Central Bastion failed completely; two Generals, Rivet and Breton, were killed; again Pélissier forbade any further attempts.

Immediately after the capture of the Malakov, a road was opened through the parallels, and an attempt was made to rush two French field batteries forward into the redoubt, to engage the works on either side. This mad act of gallantry inevitably ended in the total loss of all twelve guns, 95 out of 150 gunners and drivers, and all but 19 of the horses.

At the Redan, the British had a more difficult task; the rocky ground made it impossible to bring the last parallel nearer than 280 yards from the objective. As on 18 June, the assaulting troops came under terrific fire from the Gervais battery, and from the Barrack and Garden batteries enfilading the left flank. The inexperienced young troops straggled out of the parallel; but once they came under fire, they took cover and started to fire wildly back at the Redan. No effort on the part of their officers could move them forward; the reserves, coming behind, got hopelessly jammed in the narrow trenches. The attack eventually reached the two faces of the Redan, and there clung for three-quarters of an hour; a few brave men got inside. At last panic struck; as the Russians counter-attacked, the men turned and ran, and thus the British attack ended in a shameful rout.

No further attack could be organized, since the forward movement in the reserve trenches was jammed in hopeless confusion. Sir Colin Campbell was ordered to prepare a fresh attack on the following morning.

During the night, the troops were roused by tremendous explosions in Sevastopol. A British engineer officer crept forward to the Redan, to find it empty. A party of Highlanders was sent in to remove the wounded. At 4 am the Redan's magazine blew up, followed soon after by a huge explosion which destroyed the Flagstaff Battery.

As day broke, the Russians were seen to be filing across the bridge of boats, towards the North Side. Further explosions destroyed Fort Paul and many buildings in the town. Sevastopol, which had defied the allies for eleven months, was at last in their hands.

For the British, however, there was no rejoicing. Henry Clifford expressed the feelings of the army: 'I stood in the Redan more humble, more dejected and with a heavier heart than I have yet felt since I left home. . . . I looked towards the Malakov, there was the French flag, the Tricolor, planted on its Parapet . . . no flag floated on the Parapet on which I stood and if it had, I could have seized it, and dashed it into the ditch we could not pass, or hid it in the bosom of the young officer, dead at my feet inside the Redan.'

CHAPTER XII

The End in Asia Minor

The fall of Sevastopol finally permitted the Turkish forces to be set free for a task for which they should long ago have been released—the rescue of the allied contingents beleaguered all the summer in Kars and Erzerum.

Early in 1855, General Williams, the British officer in charge at Kars, had with his ADC, Teesdale, been trying to reorganize the defences of Kars and Erzerum. Now, he was faced with a new threat; General Bebatov, himself more than competent as a commander, had been replaced by an exceptionally skilful officer, General Muraviev. Williams was encouraged by the arrival of three more British officers, Col Lake, Maj Olpherts, and Capt Thompson; but all requests for help to allied headquarters at Balaclava and Constantinople seemed to be useless. The allied generals were too preoccupied with their own difficulties to spare a thought for the remote garrisons in Asia Minor. Appeals to Lord Clarendon, then Foreign Secretary, in London disappeared into the maw of bureaucracy. By June the garrison of Kars had only twelve days' rations left; by scraping the barrel at Erzerum, Williams succeeded in raising this amount to four months' supply.

At this time Muraviev, with about 25,000 men, including 10,000 cavalry, advanced on Kars. Williams, who was at Erzerum, hastened to Kars, where Lake had done much good work in strengthening the defences, according to plans drawn up by General Guyon. The defences, consisting of block-houses linked by breastworks, were rather too extensive to be fully manned by the garrison, whose strength was about 17,000.

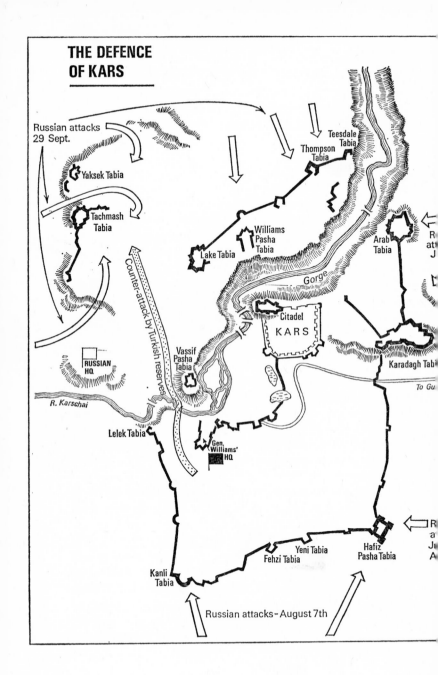

THE DEFENCE
OF KARS

Russian attacks
29 Sept.

Yaksek Tabia

Tachmash
Tabia

Counter-attack by Turkish reserves

RUSSIAN
HQ.

R. Karschai

Lelek Tabia

Lake Tabia

Williams
Pasha
Tabia

Vassif
Pasha
Tabia

Gen.
Williams'
HQ.

Gorge

Citadel

K A R S

Teesdale
Tabia

Thompson
Tabia

Arab
Tabia

Karadagh Tab

To Gu

Kanli
Tabia

Yeni Tabia
Fehzi Tabia

Hafiz
Pasha Tabia

Russian attacks – August 7th

On 16 June, Muraviev made his first attack on Kars; coming in from the east his light infantry drove in the Turkish picquets and cavalry guarding the road to Gumri. The Russian main attack consisted of three strong columns of infantry, flanked by three regiments of dragoons and supported by 48 guns.

The Russian cavalry, following the picquets to the eastern edge of the town, were driven off by the Turkish artillery in the Arab, Karadagh and Hafiz Pasha Tabias; reforming for another attack, supported by the Russian guns, they were again defeated. Muraviev was evidently surprised at the strength of the Turkish resistance, since he withdrew his troops to a distance, and settled down to besiege the city, confining his activities to skirmishes and raids to burn stores of corn and provisions. The road to Erzerum was cut; a Russian force was detailed to threaten that city early in August.

On 7 August, while Muraviev was at Erzerum, his second-in-command attempted to capture Kars. An un-imaginative attack on the south-eastern defences by massed infantry was driven off three times, without loss to the Turks.

As the garrison grew weaker Russian strength was increased; siege-guns were seen to arrive. At Erzerum an air of apathy depressed all who arrived there; at Kars on 1 September, the garrison was reduced to half rations; Williams considered that they could hold out for two months more; mutiny and desertion were rife. Information taken by spies to Muraviev caused him to choose a policy of close blockade and starvation, rather than siege warfare against the garrison.

Attempts to organize the relief of Kars proceeded with painful slowness. The Turks in Constantinople talked of sending relief from Mustafa Pasha's force at Batum, of land-ing troops at Trebizond, of sending an expedition to Redout Kaleh. In the end it was this last plan which was chosen; the force was to advance through Kutais into Georgia and against Tiflis. This move, it was felt, would afford a quicker

10

relief to Kars, than a direct attempt to raise the siege. A dispatch to this effect was sent to Omar Pasha, who approached Pélissier with a request for an immediate conference, in order to enable him to put the plan into effect, with some of the 60,000 Turkish troops in the Crimea.

At the conference, which was attended by all the commanders in the Crimea, Omar Pasha explained the situation in Asia Minor (which was unknown to the Generals)—and failing to convince them of his needs, sailed to Constantinople to confer with his government.

Stubborn opposition from both French and British in the Crimea eventually prevented Omar from getting his own way, until after the fall of Sevastopol. Omar left for the Asiatic coast on 6 September; but it was not until 29 September that Pélissier would release the Turkish troops to embark.

On that day, Muraviev changed his policy and made a determined effort to capture Kars. A massed attack on the Tachmasb defences by nearly 30,000 troops was eventually driven off by cross-fire from grape and musketry at close range. The defenders lost over 1,000 in killed and wounded, and buried 6,000 of the enemy. The attack failed mainly because the fortifications were organized for 'all-round defence'. Having turned the defences, the Russians failed to enter them, and were cut to pieces by the artillery.

On 22 October, the garrison of Kars was cheered by the news that an army of 20,000 under Selim Pasha had landed at Trebizond. Selim marched to Erzerum and halted there. However, he had no intention of relieving Kars; the pashas were preparing their revenge upon Williams, for his efforts to reveal their corruption and dishonesty.

Omar meanwhile had decided to disembark, not at Redout Kaleh, but at Sukhom Kaleh, 80 miles further to the north.

The expedition was disembarked during October; at the beginning of November, Omar, leaving garrisons at Sukhom Kaleh and Chimeharra, started to advance towards Kutais.

On 6 November, the Russians were found holding the line of the River Ingur. After a sharp battle, they were driven off, and the river crossings secured, but the Turks then delayed for 48 hours before moving on to Sugdidi. Here they delayed again for a week of beautiful weather, during which they could easily have reached Kutais. On 15 November the advance was continued, the force reaching the main road from Redout Kaleh to Kutais on 17 November. There was still no haste, no feeling of urgency. Skender Pasha, a Pole commanding the advanced guard, protested against the delay, but Omar, in reply, dawdled even more. The weather broke at last, flooding the rivers; bridges had to be rebuilt, while the army waited for another two weeks. By 3 December, their cavalry patrols reported the Russians in strength on the Skeniscal River.

Omar was too late. Had he thrust straight for Kutais, without delay, Muraviev might possibly have been forced to withdraw before Kars. On 25 November, with the last ounce of food gone and cholera breaking out, Williams had been forced to surrender Kars to Muraviev. The garrison marched out, to be honourably treated by the Russians as prisoners of war.

Shamyl had been of no help at this stage of the campaign, since his tribesmen had begun to lose their capacity for resistance. After the surrender of Kars, and the end of the Crimean War, Russia deployed larger forces in the Caucasus. Shamyl was captured in 1859 and spent the rest of his life in honourable captivity, at Kaluga, St Petersburg and Kiev. He died in 1871 while on a pilgrimage to Mecca.

CHAPTER XIII

Naval Campaigns in the Baltic, the White Sea, and the North Pacific

The Baltic campaign was reopened in the spring of 1855. In spite of the lessons learnt during the previous year, the new fleet was still lacking the small powerful gun-boats needed for work in shallow waters. Sir Charles Napier was replaced by Sir R. S. Dundas (from the Black Sea fleet). The British fleet consisted of 19 screw and one sailing ship of the line (over 60 guns), 14 frigates, 12 small steamers, 21 steam gunboats, and 15 mortar boats. To this the French added 3 ships of the line, 3 frigates, and 10 other smaller gunboats.

The fleet sailed in March, establishing once more the blockade of the Russian Baltic ports. In May reconnaissances were made to Revel, the Aland Islands, Hangö, Sveaborg and Kronstadt.

At Kronstadt, the defences were found to be much improved; attack by large ships was still out of the question. A fleet of 200 gunboats might have achieved something; but Dundas only had twenty.

At Hangö, a boat conveying ashore the crews of captured Finnish ships, under a flag of truce, was fired on by the Russians; nearly every man was killed. Both sides seem to have been to blame—the 'Massacre of Hangö' was a clear case of not keeping to the rules of war. Elsewhere a fleet of Russian coasters was destroyed at Nystad (Uusikauplinki) at the entrance to the Gulf of Bothnia, while in June, a squadron under Captain Yelverton operated with some dash against the northern coast of the Gulf of Finland. The fort of Svastholm in the Bay of Lovisa was captured, 122 guns removed and the fort blown up; at Trangsund off Viborg, the Captain found the defences too strong, but returning to Fredericksham (Hamina) the Russian fort was silenced, troops shot up, and the town set on fire.

In August, Admiral Dundas decided to bombard Sveaborg; the combined fleets were concentrated off the fortress, and on 9 August at 6.45 am, the ships opened fire. After three hours, the magazine on the principal island blew up with an enormous explosion. The bombardment was continued until 8 pm, by which time most of the British mortars were either split, or so softened as to be incapable of accurate fire. The attack was renewed on 10 and 11 August; most of the dockyards, magazines and stores were destroyed; 23 small ships were burned, and one ship of the line damaged and beached.

The rest of the Baltic campaign was confined to attacks on merchant shipping, blockade duties, and pinpricks against the Russian coastal defences. The fleet withdrew in November, while a programme of construction of 150 steam gunboats was begun, with a view to further operations in 1856; this new fleet was, however, never required.

A British squadron was sent to the White Sea, arriving in June, after unaccountable delay in starting. The remainder of the short summer was spent in harassing coastal shipping, burning stores of timber, and destroying boat-building yards.

In the Pacific, there were two British squadrons operating, one under Admiral Stirling in Chinese waters, the other, under Admiral Bruce, in the North Pacific. A third squadron, of 5 frigates, 5 sloops, and 7 steamers—in all about 300 guns—was assembled at Hong Kong, under Commodore Elliott, with the intention of acting against the Russians.

Admiral Bruce, in command since November, 1854, sent two vessels, the *Encounter* and the *Barracouta*, to watch Petropaulovsk; however, in April, under cover of fog and snow the two large Russian men-of-war and four merchant-men, which were supposed to be under observation, slipped away with the entire garrison on board. When the allied squadrons under Admiral Bruce arrived to renew the attack (which had failed under Admiral Price the previous September) they found nothing but empty buildings. The Russian squadron was making for the River Amur, which runs into the sea opposite the Sakhali Island, north of Vladivostock.

Elliott's squadron was also heading for the Amur; on the way the Russians from Petropaulovsk were found sheltering in de Castries Bay in the Gulf of Tartary.

Unwilling to attack a superior force, Elliott sent a frigate to Admiral Stirling, 1,500 miles away; instead of remaining on watch, he then followed the frigate, with the result that when Stirling's squadron returned, the Russians were gone again.

Admiral Bruce's squadron had arrived off Petropaulovsk at the same time, to find that port empty. The Russians were all safe in the Amur, which was guarded by such a tangle of shoals and sandbanks that it was impossible for the British ships to enter. The North Pacific operations were not the most notable chapter in the Navy's history!

CHAPTER XIV

The End of the War

The allies entered Sevastopol to find the city in ruins, mines exploding hourly, and cellars crammed with dead and dying. The hospital building, in the Karabel suburb, offered a spectacle so appalling that it sickened even hardened veterans, who had seen every form of suffering in the trenches and in the hospitals at Balaclava.

The allies began the task of removing the wounded, burying the dead, extracting firewood from damaged buildings and destroying the Russian dockyards and fortifications. On the North Side, the Russians strengthened the defences of the Star Fort and kept up a sporadic fire against the allied troops in Sevastopol. The British at last got on with the task of road-building, and with improvements to the railway, so that by November the transport of stores for the coming winter was assured. On 11 November, General Sir James Simpson, goaded by criticisms of his inaction, resigned his command, handing over the Army to Sir William Codrington.

Sir James has been described as amiable, honest and incompetent, not fit for the command of an army in the field, but making no pretence that he was. He retired with the 'respect, esteem, and good wishes of the Army'.

On 7 October, the Allies had dispatched a combined expedition to the mouth of the Dnieper to capture the twin forts of Kinburn and Ochakov, which guarded the entrance to the Russian naval base of Nikolayev, and to Kherson, the capital of the province.

A combined fleet of ten battleships, twenty frigates and a number of gunboats, escorted ten transports, and a special

detachment of mortar boats and three 'floating steam batteries' designed by the French. These were a new invention,
heavily armoured, and carrying guns of siege calibre.

After making a feint at Odessa, the expedition anchored
off Kinburn on 14 October. The plan of attack was for the
gunboats to sweep the beach clear of the enemy, the troops
were then to land in launches and barges towed by small
steamers of light draught, two British brigades on the right,
the artillery, sappers, cavalry, and commissariat in the centre,
and the French on the left. The British contingent was commanded by Brigadier-General Spencer, the French by
General Bazaine.

The landing was made three miles up the spit from
Kinburn fort, thus preventing the garrison from retreating,
or reinforcements from coming to its help. By 17 October
the landing force was entrenched, facing both ways, and the
French opened their first parallel 600 yards from the fort.
At 9.15 am the mortar boats and monitors opened fire,
achieving a breach in the walls by 12 noon, when the battleships then added their fire to the bombardment. When the
defence fell silent at 3 pm a cease-fire was ordered; a flag of
truce was sent in to the Governor, who agreed to surrender
the fortress and its garrison of 700 men. The following day
the Russians blew up and abandoned the fort at Ochakov.
The cavalry of the force operated cautiously a few miles
inland for the next two or three days, and then the main
body withdrew, leaving the French and a small British
detachment to repair the fort, and to garrison it as a base for
future operations.

The British Navy patrolled the mouths of the Dnieper
and the Bug until the rivers froze over in November.

Kinburn was a French project; the British would have
preferred an attack on Kaffa (Theodosia), which offered more
threat to the Russian army in the interior of the Crimea, and
to the Russian supplies which were still reaching the Crimea
from the east, by the Tongue of Arabat, and the western
shore of the Putrid Sea. As winter came, the Russians strongly

fortified the approaches to Nikolayev and Kherson; it became clear that operations from Kinburn were not practicable, and the garrison was withdrawn. The allies also withdrew all but Turkish detachments from Kertch and Eupatoria, where decorative, but ineffective, cavalry skirmishing had been the only activity.

In Sevastopol, on 15 November, a huge explosion in the former area of the French Inkerman attack, destroyed some 50 tons of powder; 80 men were killed and nearly 300 wounded; the camp was showered with shells and rockets, and the English powder-mill having been set on fire was only saved by rapid action. The explosion was caused by a French artilleryman, either playing with an unexploded Russian shell, or carelessly causing a spark when emptying a case of powder.

Skirmishing continued in the Baidar valley, used by the French as a source of firewood—otherwise the year 1855 ended with quiet on all fronts.

The new year, 1856, opened with drag-hunts, drill parades, and musketry training; the British, too late, produced a well-trained and efficient fighting force. The French army, however, deteriorated. Their fine administrative machinery which had served them so well in the first winter of the war, broke down under the strain of the increased size of their forces. Typhus and cholera took hold, and in the first three months of 1856, 53,000 patients were admitted to French hospitals in the Bosphorus, 10,000 of whom died, 90 per cent of them from typhus. In the Crimea deaths from disease exceeded 19,000 and were thought to be as high as 25,000. It was the turn of the British to help their allies— surplus clothing, tent-boards and huts were offered, together with medical aid; but most of the help was refused.

On the diplomatic front, it was Austria who at last had taken the initiative for peace. France was talking of marching against Poland through Germany; Britain had rebuilt her army in the Crimea, and was preparing for a great naval effort in the Baltic, against Kronstadt and Helsingfors;

Sardinia was suggesting that the allies should reward her efforts by increase of territory in Italy. The Austrian Government, after consulting London and Paris, on 16 December, 1855, sent Count Esterhazy on a mission to St Petersburg, with a paper stating the demands of the allies upon Russia—expressed in the terms of an ultimatum that unless the terms were accepted, Austria would come in with the allies in the war against Russia. Prussia joined in urging Russia to accept the demands.

The ultimatum made four main demands:

I Freedom of the Danubian principalities.
II Freedom of the River Danube.
III Neutralization of the Black Sea.
IV Guarantee of the rights of the Christian subjects of Turkey.

On 16 January, 1856, the Czar accepted the Austrian ultimatum—the end was in sight.

The news of the ultimatum reached Sevastopol on 24 January, where it was received with a mixture of relief by the veterans, and disappointment among the newly arrived officers, who felt that peace with Russia should not be signed until she had suffered a convincing military defeat in the field.

On 29 January, the Russian guns on the North Side suddenly opened a full-scale bombardment of the Karabel suburb, the last serious act of war by either side. Fort Nicholas was totally destroyed by the French on 4 February.

On 28 February, news came by telegraph from the Paris Peace Conference, that an armistice, lasting until 31 March, was to be declared. On the morning of 29 February, representatives of both sides met at a tent at the Traktir Bridge, to discuss the terms of the armistice. Reviews of each other's troops were arranged by both sides. On 27 April, the Treaty of Paris was finally ratified, and the war, officially, was over.

The benefits of the Crimean War were short-lived. Sevastopol was returned to the Russians, who rebuilt it; the

Russians left Asia Minor; Russian influence in the Near East was temporarily checked. Fourteen years later, the Czar repudiated the terms of the Treaty of Paris, and in 1877, war was to break out again between Russia and Turkey.

The uneasy alliance between Britain and France, which the older British Generals had found so hard to accept, lasted less than four years.

In 1859, thousands of Britons were flocking to join the Rifle Volunteers to repel the threat of a French invasion. France's naval building programme, coupled with Napoleon III's victories over the Austrians in Italy, at Magenta and Solferino, revived in Britain the image of a dominant Imperial France; while in Paris it was discovered that it was in London that the revolutionary conspirator Orsini had hatched a plot, nearly successful, to blow up the Emperor on the way to the Opera. The resultant outcry for revenge against '*perfide Albion*' stimulated recruiting in Britain, raising the strength of the Volunteers from 15,000 to 176,000 by 1861.

Britain was to stand aside from the Franco-Prussian War of 1870, and until the South African War of 1899, her army was to fight only native opponents—in Zululand in 1879, in Afghanistan from 1878 to 1880, in the Sudan in 1884 and Egypt in 1896.

The Crimean War stood on a watershed between old-fashioned methods and weapons, and modern twentieth-century warfare. During or immediately after the war many new inventions were to be brought into general use—rifled small arms and artillery, elongated bullets and shells, the electric telegraph, leading to the field telephone; the railway, and the iron-clad warship.

In tactics, mass formations of both cavalry and infantry were to be abandoned in favour of more open and flexible formations, relying on greater fire-power.

In organization, the specialist administrative corps were to grow up; there was to be a huge improvement in medical services; the system of staff, command, and the training of officers was to be improved. The Duke of Wellington's method of selecting officers by their social connections was discredited; the prejudice against officers of experience—the 'Indian officers'—was gradually to disappear. In the Indian Mutiny of 1857, officers with Crimean experience were to lead their men with skill, and with a new-found consideration for the welfare of their troops. Admiration for the Prussian system, so successful against the French in 1870, was to give further impetus to the reforms of the British Army, instituted by Cardwell.

The old Duke of Cambridge presided over all these changes until 1895; in this time the purchase of commissions was abolished; flogging was ended; the 'short service' system of six years with the colours and six with the reserve was introduced. The Duke, however, was one of the old school, and in many ways acted as a brake against progress, regarding reforms with suspicion, and persisting in promotion by seniority rather than by ability.

The momentum of many lessons learnt in the Crimea was gradually lost. The British were to learn field-craft again the hard way—against the Boer commandos.

The battlefields of the Crimea are closed to tourists at present—Sevastopol is still a naval base forbidden even to Russian visitors. Perhaps the day will come when we shall again be able to wander on the Sapouné Heights, to stand on the knoll at Kadikoi, to look down upon the Redan, or to search for a trace of the Sandbag Battery. If that day comes, it is hoped that this small work will help the traveller to find his way back into the past.

Chronological Table

1853

March	2	Menshikov arrives in Constantinople with demands on the Porte.
May	21	Menshikov leaves Constantinople, breaking off relations.
	31	Russian ultimatum to Turkey.
June	8	British fleet approaches Dardanelles.
July	2	Russian army crosses the Pruth into Moldavia.
Oct	5	Turkey declares war on Russia.
	28	Turkish army crosses the Danube at Kalafat.
	30	British fleet enters the Bosphorus.
Nov	4	Russians defeated by Turks at Oltenitza.
	30	Turkish naval squadron destroyed at Sinope.

1854

Jan	4	Allied fleets enter the Black Sea.
	5	Turks win battle of Citate.
	8	Russians invade the Dobruja.
Feb	10	British peace deputation sees the Czar.
	23	The Guards leave England.
March	11	Baltic fleet leaves Spithead.
	19	French troops sail for Turkey.
	20	French Baltic fleet sails.
	28	France and Great Britain declare war on Russia.
April	5	British arrive at Gallipoli.

April	14	Russians besiege Silistra.
	18	Turkish victory at Rahova.
	20	Austria and Prussia declare their neutrality.
	22	Bombardment of Odessa.
May	28	Embarkation of Allied force for Varna.
June	23	Russians abandon the siege of Silistra.
	26	Allied fleet arrives off Kronstadt.
July	7	Russians defeated at Giurgevo.
	28	Russians withdraw across Pruth.
	28	Russians defeat Turks at Bayezid in Asia Minor.
Aug	13	Allies besiege Bomarsund.
	16	Surrender of Bomarsund.
	21	Bombardment of Kola, in the White Sea, by British squadron.
	30	British naval failure at Petropaulovsk.
Sept	5	Allies embark at Varna for Crimea.
	14	Landing at Calamita Bay.
	19	Encounter at River Bulganek.
	20	Battle of Alma.
	23	Russian fleet scuttled in Sevastopol.
	24	Arrival of Col Williams at Kars.
		'Flank march' of the Allies round Sevastopol.
	26	British arrive at Balaclava.
	29	Death of St Arnaud.
Oct	12	*Times* Fund originated.
	13	Patriotic Fund originated.
	17	First Bombardment of Sevastopol.
	23	Departure of Florence Nightingale and 38 nurses from England.
	25	Battle of Balaclava.
	26	Russian attack of 'Little Inkerman'.
Nov	5	Battle of Inkerman.
		Florence Nightingale arrives at Scutari.
	14	Hurricane in Crimea.
Dec	22	Sir Edmund Lyons replaces Admiral Dundas as commander of British fleet.

Dec	24	Admiral Bruat succeeds Admiral Hamelin in command of French fleet.

1855

Jan	10	Russian feint attack on Balaclava.
	17	Russian attack on Eupatoria.
	26	Sardinia joins the Allies.
	31	Fall of Lord Aberdeen's government.
Feb	5	Lord Palmerston forms new government.
	20	Allied attack across Chernaya frustrated by snowstorm.
	22	Russians seize and fortify the Mamelon.
	24	French attack on 'White Works' defeated.
March	2	Death of Czar Nicholas I, succession of Alexander II, who recalls Menshikov.
	15	Vienna conference opens.
April	4	Second Baltic expedition leaves Spithead.
	9	Second Bombardment of Sevastopol.
	26	Vienna conference closes, without result.
May	1	Fierce fighting on the French left, at the Quarantine Cemetery.
	2	First expedition sails for Kertch and is recalled by Canrobert.
	16	Canrobert resigns command of French army and is succeeded by Pélissier.
	23	Expedition to Kertch sails again.
	25	Capture of Kertch and Yenikale.
	26	Allied naval forces enter Sea of Azov.
June	5	'Massacre' of boats' crew at Hangö.
	6	Third Bombardment of Sevastopol.
		Capture of the 'White Works', the Mamelon and The Quarries by the Allies.
	16	First Russian attack at Kars.
	17	Fourth Bombardment of Sevastopol.

June	18	Main assault on the Malakov and Redan defeated with heavy loss.
	28	Death of Lord Raglan.
July	1	General Sir James Simpson appointed to command British army.
	14	Conference at which Omar Pasha asks permission to withdraw troops for Asia Minor.
Aug	7	Second Russian attack at Kars.
	9	Bombardment of Sveaborg.
	16	Russian attack at Battle of Chernaya defeated by French and Sardinian forces.
	17	Fifth Bombardment of Sevastopol.
Sept	5	Sixth Bombardment of Sevastopol.
	6	Omar Pasha leaves for Asia Minor.
	8	Attack on Malakov by French is successful.
		French fail at Little Redan and Bastion du Mât.
		British fail at the Redan.
	9	Russians evacuate South Side of Sevastopol.
	29	Russian attack at Kars defeated.
		Cavalry skirmishing at Eupatoria.
		Omar Pasha's troops embark for Asia Minor.
Oct	3	Omar Pasha lands at Suchum Kaleh, with expedition for relief of Kars.
	7	Kinburn expedition sails.
	17	Allied expedition captures Kinburn, Ochakov evacuated.
	22	Selim Pasha's army lands at Trebizond and marches to Erzerum.
Nov	6	Omar Pasha defeats Russians on River Ingur.
	11	Sir James Simpson resigns, succeeded by Sir William Codrington.
	15	French magazine at Sevastopol explodes.
	25	Surrender of Kars.
Dec	8	Omar Pasha's army forced to withdraw from River Skeniscal.

Dec 16   Count Esterhazy takes Austria's ultimatum to
              St Petersburg.

1856

Jan	16	The Czar accepts the Austrian demands.
	29	Russian guns bombard Sevastopol.
Feb	25	Paris Peace Conference opens.
	29	Armistice in the Crimea.
March	30	Treaty of Paris signed.
April	27	Ratification of Treaty of Paris, formal end of the war.

APPENDIX II

Bibliography

A list, by no means complete, of some of the more important British, French and Russian sources of information.

Adye, John   *A review of the Crimean War to the winter of 1854–1855.* London, 1860.
Notes by a British Lieutenant-Colonel, who fought in the war.

Bapst, Constant Germain   *Le Maréchal Canrobert: Souvenirs d'un Siècle.* 6 vols. Paris, 1898–1912.
Personal reminiscences, letters and documents of Canrobert.

Bazancourt, C. L., Baron de   *Cinq mois devant Sébastopol. L'Expédition de Crimée jusqu'à la pris de Sébastopol.* Paris, 1855.
Account by literary man sent by Napoleon III to record events in the Crimea.

Bonner Smith, D. and Dewar, A. C.   *Russian War 1854. Baltic and Black Sea Official Correspondence.* London, 1943.
Edited collection of Admiralty correspondence.

Bosquet, P. F. J.   *Lettres du Maréchal Bosquet 1830–1858.* Paris, 1894.
Lettres du Maréchal Bosquet à sa Mère. 4 Vols. Pau, 1877–1879.
Lettres du Maréchal Bosquet à ses Amis 1837–1860. 2 Vols. Pau, 1879.

Important correspondence about the campaign in Algeria and the Crimean War.

Brackenbury, G. *The Campaign in the Crimea.* 2 Vols. London, 1855–1856.
Chiefly valuable for its detailed description of the full series of prints by W. Simpson illustrating the war.

Buzzard, Surgeon T. *With the Turkish Army in the Crimea and Asia Minor.* London, 1915.

Calthorpe, S. J. G. *Letters from Headquarters.* 2 Vols. London, 1857.
Valuable account by a member of Raglan's staff.

Campbell, Colin Frederick *Letters from Camp to his Relatives during the Siege of Sevastopol.* London, 1894.
Eye-witness account by a British Captain, not to be confused with Sir Colin Campbell, commander of the Highland Brigade. Fierce indictment of Raglan and British administration.

Cardigan, Earl of *Eight months on active service.* London, 1856.

Castellane, Esprit V. E. B., Maréchal Comte de *Campagnes de Crimée, d'Italie, d'Afrique, de Chine, et de Mexique 1848–1862.* Paris, 1898.
Letters to Marshal de Castellane from d'Hilliers, Niel, Bosquet, Pélissier, Canrobert, Levaillant and others.
Journal du Maréchal de Castellane 1804–1862. 5 Vols. Paris, 1897.
Important French source.

Cler, J. J. G. *Reminiscences of an Officer of Zouaves.* New York, 1860.
Author fought as a Colonel and later a

General, with the Zouaves in Africa and the Crimea.

Includes account of the march from Gallipoli to Varna.

Clifford, Henry   *Henry Clifford V.C. His Letters and Sketches from the Crimea.* Toronto, 1956.

Excellent eyewitness account, with amateur but very graphic watercolour illustrations.

Collection des Ordres Generaux de l'Armée d'Orient. 1854–1856.

French general orders for the campaign.

General Orders of the Army of the East 1854–1856.

British general orders for the campaign.

Delafield, Richard   *Report of Major Richard Delafield.* Washington, 1860.

Report of the U.S. Military Commission sent to inspect the war in Europe. Technical reports on engineers, cavalry and ordnance.

Douglas, G. and Ramsay, G. D.   *The Panmure Papers.* 2 Vols. London, 1908.

Lord Panmure was Secretary of State for War in Palmerston's cabinet. Letters and dispatches from Raglan, Palmerston, Clarendon, and others.

Duberly, Frances Isabella   *Journal kept during the Russian War.* London, 1855 and 1963.

The wife of a British officer, Mrs Duberly accompanied the expedition to Varna, and to Balaclava.

Earp, G. B.   *The History of the Baltic Campaign of 1854.* London, 1857.

Documents and letters provided by Admiral Sir Charles Napier.

Elphinstone, H. C. and Jones, H. D.   *Journal of Operations*

conducted by the Corps of Royal Engineers in the Crimea. London, 1859.
Eyewitness account by two generals.

Fenton, R   *Roger Fenton, Photographer of the Crimean War.* London, 1954.

Filder, C. B.   *The Commissariat in the Crimea.* London, 1856.
The Commissary-General's reply to criticisms by the Commission of Enquiry.

Fortescue, J. W.   *A History of the British Army.* 13 Vols. London, 1889–1930.
Material for the Crimean War taken from Kinglake, Bazancourt, Hamley, Todleben, and French Archives.

Gooch, Brison D.   *The New Bonapartist Generals in the Crimean War.* The Hague, 1959.
American account of the war from the French point of view. Excellent survey, uncluttered by tactical details; no maps or illustrations. Very good bibliography.

Hamley, Edward Bruce   *The Campaign of Sevastopol.* London, 1855.
Operations of War. London, 1878.
The War in the Crimea. London, 1891.
Author, a British general, fought as a junior officer in the Crimea. Straightforward clear account.

Heath, Leopold George   *Letters from the Black Sea during the Crimean War.* London, 1897.
Eyewitness account by a British admiral.

Hibbert, Christopher   *The Destruction of Lord Raglan.* London, 1961.
Sympathetic and interesting defence of Lord Raglan.

Hodasevich, R. A.   *A Voice from within the Walls of Sevastopol.* London, 1856.

Interesting account by a Polish officer who defected from the Russians. Inaccurate battle maps.

Hume, S. R. *Reminiscences of the Crimean Campaign.* London, 1894.
Diary and letters by a Major-General who fought in the Crimea as a junior officer.

Kinglake, A. W. *The Invasion of the Crimea.* 8 Vols. London, 1863–1887.
The author, a literary man, accompanied Raglan to the Crimea, and wrote this work later at the request of his family. Though used for a long time as the standard work on the war, it is very incomplete as a history, since it ends with Raglan's death, and is very biased against the French. Superb maps and diagrams.

Lake, A. *Kars and our Captivity in Russia.* London, 1856.
Letters from British Officers, about the Campaign in Asia Minor.

La Motte Rouge, J. E. de *Souvenirs et Campagnes.* Paris, 1895–1898.
Reminiscences of one of the leading French generals in the Crimea.

Lane-Poole, S. *Life of Stratford Canning, Viscount Stratford de Redcliffe.* 2 Vols. London, 1888.

Lysons, Daniel *The Crimean War from First to Last.* London, 1895.
Eyewitness account by a British General who fought as a junior officer in the Crimea.

MacMahon, M. de *Mémoires du Maréchal MacMahon, Duc de Magenta.* Paris, 1932.
Author commanded a division in the Crimea.

MacMunn, G.   *The Crimea in Perspective.* London, 1935.
A retrospective survey, based largely on Kinglake.

Marriott, J. A. R.   *The Eastern Question.* Oxford, 1940.
A study in European diplomacy.

Marx, Karl   *The Eastern Question.* London, 1897.
Includes letters written 1853–1856 dealing with the Crimean War.

Mitra, S. M.   *The Life and Letters of Sir John Hall.* London, 1911.
Memoranda and diaries of a senior medical officer in the Crimea.

Niel, Adolphe   *Siège de Sébastopol; Journal des Operations du Genie.* Paris, 1858.
Day-to-day account of the siege by the author, a senior engineer officer sent by Napoleon III to watch the conduct of affairs in the Crimea by Canrobert.

Nolan, E. H.   *The History of the War against Russia.* 2 Vols. London, 1857.
A very full history of the war, including all other theatres besides the Crimea. A mass of detail, including biographies, correspondence and dispatches. Illustrations of little value, maps poor, orders of battle inaccurate.

Paget, George A. F.   *Extracts from the Letters and Journal of Lord George Paget during the Crimean War.* London, 1881.
Author was second-in-command of the Light Brigade during the Charge. Much recrimination about the failure of the reserve regiments under his command to keep in touch.

Peard, G. S.   *Campaign in the Crimea.* London, 1855.
Journal by a lieutenant who fought at

Alma, Balaclava and Inkerman; July 1854 to January 1855.

Quatrelle l'Epine, M. *Le Maréchal de Saint Arnaud. 1798–1854.*

An important biography of St Arnaud.

Reid, A. D. *Memories of the Crimean War.* London, 1911.

Letters from a surgeon.

Robbins, M. 'The Balaclava Railway'. *Journal of Transport History I* (1953) and *II* (1955).

Technical monograph, interesting to railway-lovers.

Robinson, Frederick *Diary of the Crimean War.* London, 1856.

Another surgeon's diary.

Ross-of-Bladensburg, J. F. G. *The Coldstream Guards in the Crimea.* London, 1897.

Rousset, Camille *Histoire de le Guerre Crimée.* 2 Vols. Paris, 1897.

Important French source.

Russell, W. H. *Complete History of the Crimean War.* New York, 1856.

War correspondent's account from the Crimea.

General Todleben's History of the Defence of Sevastopol.

Heavily edited version, revealing little of what Todleben actually wrote.

The British Expedition to the Crimea. London, 1858.

The War. London, 1855.

Sandwith, Humphrey *A Narrative of the Siege of Kars.* London, 1856.

Sayer, Frederick *Despatches and letters relative to the Crimean War.* London, 1857. Edited official British, and some French dispatches.

Shadwell, L. *The Life of Colin Campbell, Lord Clyde.* 2 Vols. London, 1881.

Sterling, A. C.   *The Highland Brigade in the Crimea.* London, 1895. Good critical account by an officer on the Highland Brigade Staff.

Todleben, Eduard Ivanovich   *Défense de Sébastopol.* 2 Vols. St Petersburg, 1863–1874.

Tolstoy, Leo   *Sevastopol Sketches*—1852–1889. Author fought in the Crimea.

Tulloch, A. M.   *The Crimean Commission and the Chelsea Board.* London, 1857. Author a member of the original commission. Useful statistics.

Vulliamy, C. E.   *Crimea.* London, 1939.

Willesley, F. A.   *The Paris Embassy during the Second Empire.* London, 1928. Author the son of Lord Cowley, Ambassador to France during the Crimean War. *Secrets of the Second Empire.* *Conversations with Napoleon III.*

Windham, Sir C. A.   *Crimean Diary and Letters*, ed. Major Pearse, London, 1897. Author commanded a brigade in the Crimea.

Wood, Sir Evelyn   *The Crimea in 1854 and 1894.* London, 1895. Excellent retrospective account. Author fought as a midshipman in the Naval Brigade, and later transferred to the Army, rising to the rank of Field-Marshal.

Woodham-Smith, Cecil   *Florence Nightingale.* London, 1950. Full definitive biography. *The Reason Why.* London, 1953. Analysis of the characters of Lords Lucan and Cardigan, leading to the disaster at Balaclava.

Wrottesley, George *Life and Letters of Sir John Burgoyne.*
London, 1873.
Author was Burgoyne's son-in-law.
*The Military Opinions of Sir John Fox
Burgoyne.* London, 1859.
Regimental Histories.   A complete list of regiments of the
British Army taking part in the Crimea
can be found in Appendix III and IV.

APPENDIX III

The British Cavalry

(Regiments in italics served in the Crimea)

Title 1854	*Title 1900*	*Title 1971*
1st Life Guards	1st Life Guards	The Life Guards
2nd Life Guards	2nd Life Guards	
Royal Horse Guards	Royal Horse Guards	The Blues & Royals
1st (King's) Dragoon Guards	1st (King's) Dragoon Guards	1st Queen's Dragoon Guards
2nd Queen's Dragoon Guards	2nd Dragoon Guards (Queen's Bays)	1st Queen's Dragoon Guards
3rd (Prince of Wales's) Dragoon Guards	3rd (Prince of Wales's) Dragoon Guards	Royal Scots Dragoon Guards (Carabiniers & Greys)
4th Royal Irish Dragoon Guards	4th Royal Irish Dragoon Guards	4th/7th Royal Dragoon Guards
5th (Princess Charlotte of Wales's) Dragoon Guards	5th (Princess Charlotte of Wales's) Dragoon Guards	5th Royal Inniskilling Dragoon Guards
6th Dragoon Guards (Carabiniers)	6th Dragoon Guards (Carabiniers)	Royal Scots Dragoon Guards (Carabiniers & Greys)
7th (Princess Royal's) Dragoon Guards	7th (Princess Royal's) Dragoon Guards	4th/7th Royal Dragoon Guards
1st (Royal) Dragoons	1st (Royal) Dragoons	The Blues & Royals
2nd Royal North British Dragoons (Scots Greys)	2nd Dragoons (Royal Scots Greys)	Royal Scots Dragoon Guards (Carabiniers & Greys)
3rd (King's Own) Light Dragoons	3rd (King's Own) Hussars	Queen's Own Hussars
4th (Queen's Own) Light Dragoons	4th (Queen's Own) Hussars	Queen's Royal Irish Hussars
5th (Royal Irish) Dragoons [disbanded 1799 until 1861, when reraised]	5th (Royal Irish) Lancers	16th/5th Queen's Royal Lancers

6th (*Inniskilling*) *Dragoons*	6th (Inniskilling) Dragoons	5th Royal Inniskilling Dragoon Guards
7th (Queen's Own) Light Dragoons (Hussars)	7th Queen's Own Hussars	Queen's Own Hussars
8th *King's Royal Irish* (*Light*) *Dragoons* (*Hussars*)	8th (King's Royal Irish) Hussars	Queen's Royal Irish Hussars
9th (Queen's Royal) Light Dragoons (Lancers)	9th (Queen's Royal) Lancers	9th/12th Royal Lancers (Prince of Wales's)
10th (*Prince of Wales's Own Royal*) *Light Dragoons* (*Hussars*)	10th (Prince of Wales's Own) Hussars	The Royal Hussars (Prince of Wales's Own)
11th (*Prince Albert's Own*) *Hussars*	11th (Prince Albert's Own) Hussars	The Royal Hussars (Prince of Wales's Own)
12th (*Prince of Wales's Royal*) *Lancers*	12th (Prince of Wales's Royal) Lancers	9th/12th Royal Lancers (Prince of Wales's)
13th *Light Dragoons*	13th Hussars	13th/18th Royal Hussars (Queen Mary's Own)
14th (King's) Light Dragoons	14th (King's) Hussars	14th/20th King's Hussars
15th (King's) Light Dragoons (Hussars)	15th (King's) Hussars	15th/19th King's Royal Hussars
16th (Queen's) Light Dragoons (Lancers)	16th (Queen's) Lancers	16th/5th Queen's Royal Lancers
17th *Light Dragoons* (*Lancers*)	17th (Duke of Cambridge's Own) Lancers	17th/21st Lancers

Regiments re-raised in 1858

18th Light Dragoons (Hussars) (disbanded 1821)	18th Hussars	13th/18th Royal Hussars (Queen Mary's Own)
19th Light Dragoons (disbanded 1821)	19th (Princess of Wales's Own) Hussars	15th/19th King's Royal Hussars
20th Light Dragoons (disbanded 1819)	20th Hussars	14th/20th King's Hussars
20th Light Dragoons (disbanded 1819)	21st (Empress of India's) Lancers	17th/21st Lancers

The British Infantry

(Regiments in italics served in the Crimea)

Title 1854	*Title 1900*	*Title 1971*
Grenadier Guards	Grenadier Guards	Grenadier Guards
Coldstream Guards	Coldstream Guards	Coldstream Guards
Scots Fusilier Guards	Scots Guards	Scots Guards
—	Irish Guards (1902)	Irish Guards
—	—	Welsh Guards (1914)
1st Foot	Royal Scots	Royal Scots
2nd ,,	Queen's (Royal West Surrey Regt)	Queen's Regiment
3rd ,,	Buffs (East Kent Regt)	Queen's Regiment
4th ,,	King's Own (Royal Lancaster Regt)	King's Own Royal Border Regt
5th ,,	Northumberland Fusiliers	Royal Regiment of Fusiliers
6th ,,	Royal Warwickshire Regt	Royal Regiment of Fusiliers
7th ,,	Royal Fusiliers	Royal Regiment of Fusiliers
8th ,,	King's (Liverpool Regt)	King's Regt
9th ,,	Norfolk Regt	(1st Bn) Royal Anglian Regt
10th ,,	Lincolnshire Regt	(2nd Bn) Royal Anglian Regt
11th ,,	Devonshire Regt	Devonshire & Dorset Regt
12th ,,	Suffolk Regt	(1st Bn) Royal Anglian Regt
13th ,,	Prince Albert's (Somersetshire Light Infantry)	Light Infantry
14th ,,	Prince of Wales's Own (West Yorkshire Regt)	Prince of Wales's Own Regiment of Yorkshire

15th Foot	East Yorkshire Regt	Prince of Wales's Own Regiment of Yorkshire
16th „	Bedfordshire Regt	(3rd Bn) Royal Anglian Regt
17th „	Leicestershire Regt	(4th Bn) Royal Anglian Regt
18th „	Royal Irish Regt	Disbanded 1922
19th „	Princess of Wales's Own (Yorkshire Regt)	Green Howards
20th „	Lancashire Fusiliers	Royal Regiment of Fusiliers
21st „	Royal Scots Fusiliers	Royal Highland Fusiliers
22nd „	Cheshire Regt	Cheshire Regt
23rd „	Royal Welsh Fusiliers	Royal Welch Fusiliers
24th „	South Wales Borderers	Royal Regiment of Wales
25th „	King's Own Scottish Borderers	King's Own Scottish Borderers
26th „	(1st Bn) Cameronians (Scottish Rifles)	Disbanded 1968
27th „	(1st Bn) Royal Inniskilling Fusiliers	Royal Irish Rangers
28th „	(1st Bn) Gloucestershire Regt	Gloucestershire Regt
29th „	(1st Bn) Worcestershire Regt	Worcestershire & Sherwood Foresters Regt
30th „	(1st Bn) East Lancashire Regt	Queen's Lancashire Regt
31st „	(1st Bn) East Surrey Regt	Queen's Regt
32nd „	(1st Bn) Duke of Cornwall's Light Infantry	Light Infantry
33rd „	(1st Bn) Duke of Wellington's West Riding Regt	Duke of Wellington's Regt
34th „	(1st Bn) Border Regt	King's Own Royal Border Regt
35th „	(1st Bn) Royal Sussex Regt	Queen's Regt
36th „	(2nd Bn) Worcestershire Regt	Worcestershire & Sherwood Foresters Regt

37th Foot	(1st Bn) Hampshire Regt	Royal Hampshire Regt
38th ,,	(1st Bn) South Staffordshire Regt	Staffordshire Regt
39th ,,	(1st Bn) Dorsetshire Regt	Devonshire & Dorset Regt
40th ,,	(1st Bn) Prince of Wales's Volunteers (South Lancashire Regt)	Queen's Lancashire Regt
41st ,,	(1st Bn) Welsh Regt	Royal Regiment of Wales
42nd ,,	(1st Bn) Black Watch (Royal Highlanders)	Black Watch (Royal Highland Regt)
43rd ,,	(1st Bn) Oxfordshire Light Infantry	(1st Bn) Royal Green Jackets
44th ,,	(1st Bn) Essex Regt	(3rd Bn) Royal Anglian Regt
45th ,,	(1st Bn) Sherwood Foresters (Derbyshire) Regt	Worcestershire & Sherwood Foresters Regt
46th ,,	(2nd Bn) Duke of Cornwall's Light Infantry	Light Infantry
47th ,,	(1st Bn) Loyal North Lancashire Regt	Queen's Lancashire Regt
48th ,,	(1st Bn) Northampton-shire Regt	(2nd Bn) Royal Anglian Regt
49th ,,	(1st Bn) Princess Charlotte of Wales's (Royal Berkshire Regt)	Duke of Edinburgh's Royal Regt
50th	(1st Bn) Queen's Own (Royal West Kent Regt)	Queen's Regt
51st ,,	(1st Bn) King's Own (Yorkshire Light Infantry)	Light Infantry
52nd ,,	(2nd Bn) Oxfordshire Light Infantry	(1st Bn) Royal Green Jackets
53rd ,,	(1st Bn) King's (Shropshire Light Infantry)	Light Infantry
54th ,,	(2nd Bn) Dorsetshire Regt	Devonshire & Dorset Regt
55th ,,	(2nd Bn) Border Regt	King's Own Royal Border Regt

56th Foot	(2nd Bn) Essex Regt	(3rd Bn) Royal Anglian Regt
57th ,,	(1st Bn) Duke of Cambridge's Own (Middlesex Regt)	Queen's Regt
58th ,,	(2nd Bn) Northamptonshire Regt	(2nd Bn) Royal Anglian Regt
59th ,,	(2nd Bn) East Lancaster Regt	Queen's Lancashire Regt
60th ,,	King's Royal Rifle Corps	(2nd Bn) Royal Green Jackets
61st ,,	(2nd Bn) Gloucestershire Regt	Gloucestershire Regt
62nd ,,	(1st Bn) Duke of Edinburgh's (Wiltshire Regt)	Duke of Edinburgh's Royal Regt
63rd ,,	(1st Bn) Manchester Regt	King's Regt
64th ,,	(1st Bn) Prince of Wales's (North Staffordshire Regt)	Staffordshire Regt
65th ,,	(1st Bn) York & Lancaster Regt	Disbanded 1968
66th ,,	(2nd Bn) Princess Charlotte of Wales's (Royal Berkshire Regt)	Duke of Edinburgh's Royal Regt
67th ,,	(2nd Bn) Hampshire Regt	Royal Hampshire Regt
68th ,,	(1st Bn) Durham Light Infantry	Light Infantry
69th ,,	(2nd Bn) Welsh Regt	Royal Regt of Wales
70th ,,	(2nd Bn) East Surrey Regt	Queen's Regt
71st ,,	(1st Bn) Highland Light Infantry	Royal Highland Fusiliers
72nd ,,	(1st Bn) Seaforth Highlanders	Queen's Own Highlanders
73rd ,,	(2nd Bn) Black Watch (Royal Highlanders)	Black Watch (Royal Highland Regt)
74th ,,	(2nd Bn) Highland Light Infantry	Royal Highland Fusiliers
75th ,,	(1st Bn) Gordon Highlanders	Gordon Highlanders
76th ,,	(2nd Bn) Duke of Wellington's (West Riding Regt)	Duke of Wellington's Regt

77th Foot	(2nd Bn) Duke of Cambridge's Own (Middlesex Regt)	Queen's Regt
78th ,,	(2nd Bn) Seaforth Highlanders	Queen's Own Highlanders
79th ,,	(1st Bn) Queen's Own Cameron Highlanders	Queen's Own Highlanders
80th ,,	(2nd Bn) South Staffordshire Regt	Staffordshire Regt
81st ,,	(2nd Bn) Loyal North Lancashire Regt	Queen's Lancashire Regt
82nd ,,	(2nd Bn) Prince of Wales's Volunteers (South Lancashire Regt)	Queen's Lancashire Regt
83rd ,,	(1st Bn) Royal Irish Rifles	Royal Irish Rangers
84th ,,	(2nd Bn) York & Lancaster Regt	Disbanded 1968
85th ,,	(2nd Bn) King's (Shropshire Light Infantry)	Light Infantry
86th ,,	(2nd Bn) Royal Irish Rifles	Royal Irish Rangers
87th ,,	(1st Bn) Princess Victoria's (Royal Irish Fusiliers)	Royal Irish Rangers
88th ,,	(1st Bn) Connaught Rangers	Disbanded 1922
89th ,,	(2nd Bn) Princess Victoria's (Royal Irish Fusiliers)	Royal Irish Rangers
90th ,,	(2nd Bn) Cameronians (Scottish Rifles)	Disbanded 1968
91st ,,	(1st Bn) Princess Louise's (Argyll & Sutherland Highlanders)	Argyll & Sutherland Highlanders
92nd ,,	(2nd Bn) Gordon Highlanders	Gordon Highlanders
93rd ,,	(2nd Bn) Princess Louise's (Argyll & Sutherland Highlanders)	Argyll & Sutherland Highlanders
94th ,,	(2nd Bn) Connaught Rangers	Disbanded 1922

12

95th Foot	(2nd Bn) Sherwood Foresters (Derbyshire) Regt	Worcestershire & Sherwood Foresters Regt
96th ,,	(2nd Bn) Manchester Regt	The King's Regt
97th ,,	(2nd Bn) Queen's Own (Royal West Kent Regt)	Queen's Regt
98th ,,	(2nd Bn) Prince of Wales's (North Staffordshire Regt)	Staffordshire Regt
99th ,,	(2nd Bn) Duke of Edinburgh's (Wiltshire Regt)	Duke of Edinburgh's Royal Regt
Rifle Brigade	Rifle Brigade (Prince Consort's Own)	(3rd Bn) Royal Green Jackets

Regiments formed after 1854

100th Foot	(1st Bn) Prince of Wales's Leinster Regt	Disbanded 1922
101st ,,	(1st Bn) Royal Munster Fusiliers	Disbanded 1922
102nd ,,	(1st Bn) Royal Dublin Fusiliers	Disbanded 1922
103rd ,,	(2nd Bn) Royal Dublin Fusiliers	Disbanded 1922
104th ,,	(2nd Bn) Royal Munster Fusiliers	Disbanded 1922
105th ,,	(2nd Bn) King's Own (Yorkshire Light Infantry)	Light Infantry
106th ,,	(2nd Bn) Durham Light Infantry	Light Infantry
107th ,,	(2nd Bn) Royal Sussex Regt	Queen's Regt
108th ,,	(2nd Bn) Royal Inniskilling Fusiliers	Royal Irish Rangers
109th ,,	(2nd Bn) Prince of Wales's Leinster Regt	Disbanded 1922

British Orders of Battle

1. BRITISH EXPEDITIONARY FORCE AT VARNA, 1854

1st Division
(Duke of Cambridge)

1st Bde (Bentinck)
   Grenadier Guards
   Coldstream Guards
   Scots Fusilier Guards
2nd Bde (Sir Colin Campbell)
   42nd, 79th, 93rd

2nd Division
(Sir George de Lacy
Evans)

1st Bde (Pennefather) 30th, 55th,
   95th
2nd Bde (Adams) 41st, 47th, 49th

3rd Division
(Sir Richard England)

1st Bde (Eyre) 1st, 38th, 50th
2nd Bde (Sir John Campbell) 4th,
   28th, 44th

4th Division
(Sir George Cathcart)

1st Bde (Goldie) 20th, 21st, 1st
   Bn Rifle Bde
2nd Bde (Torrens) 63rd, 45th, 57th

Light Division
(Sir George Brown)

1st Bde (Airey, then Codrington)
2nd Bn Rifle Bde, 7th, 23rd, 33rd

Cavalry Division
(The Earl of Lucan)

Light Brigade (The Earl of
   Cardigan)
   4th Light Dragoons
   8th King's Royal Irish Hussars
   11th Hussars
   13th Light Dragoons
   17th Lancers

Heavy Brigade (Scarlett)
  1st Dragoons (The Royals)
  2nd Dragoons (Scots Greys)
  4th Dragoon Guards
    (Royal Irish)
  5th Dragoon Guards
  6th Dragoons (Inniskilling)

2. BRITISH ARMY IN THE CRIMEA, JULY, 1855

1st Division
(Lord Rokeby)

1st Bde (Crauford)
  Grenadier Guards
  Coldstream Guards
  Scots Fusilier Guards
2nd Bde (Ridley) 9th, 13th, 31st,
  2nd Bn Rifle Bde

Highland Division
(Sir Colin Campbell)

1st Bde (Cameron) 42nd, 79th,
  93rd
2nd Bde (Horn) 1st and 2nd Bns
  1st Foot, 71st, 90th

2nd Division
(Markham)

1st Bde (Warren) 3rd, 30th, 55th,
  95th
2nd Bde (Windham) 41st, 47th,
  49th, 62nd

3rd Division
(England, till August,
  then Eyre)

1st Bde (Barlow) 4th, 14th, 39th,
  50th, 89th
2nd Bde (Trollope) 18th, 28th,
  38th, 44th

4th Division
(Bentinck)

1st Bde (Spencer) 17th, 20th, 21st,
  57th, 63rd
2nd Bde (Garrett) 46th, 48th, 68th,
  1st Bn Rifle Bde

Light Division
(Codrington)

1st Bde (Straubenzee) 7th, 23rd,
  33rd, 34th
2nd Bde (Shirley) 19th, 77th, 88th,
  97th

Cavalry Division
(Scarlett)

Light Bde (Paget)
    4th, 13th Light Dragoons
    12th Lancers
    6th Dragoon Guards
Hussar Bde (Parlby) 8th, 10th,
    11th Hussars, 17th Lancers
Heavy Bde (Lawrenson) 1st, 4th,
    5th Dragoon Guards
    1st, 2nd, 6th Dragoons

French Orders of Battle

Army HQ (St Arnaud)	Chief of Staff, de Martimprey ADC Trochu
1st Division (Canrobert)	1st Bde (Espinasse) 4th Chasseurs, 1st Zouaves, 7th de Ligne 2nd Bde (Vinoy) 9th Chasseurs, 20th de Ligne, 27th de Ligne
2nd Division (Bosquet)	1st Bde (D'Autemarre) Tirailleurs, 3rd Zouaves, 50th de Ligne 2nd Bde (Bouat) 3rd Chasseurs, 7th Léger, 6th de Ligne
3rd Division (Prince Napoleon)	1st Bde (Monet) 2nd Zouaves, Marine Regiment 2nd Bde (Thomas) 22nd Léger
4th Division (Forey)	1st Bde (de Lourmel) 5th Chasseurs, 19th, 26th de Ligne 2nd Bde (Aurelle) 39th, 74th de Ligne
Cavalry Brigade (D'Allonville)	1st Chasseurs d'Afrique 4th Chasseurs d'Afrique
Cavalry Brigade (Cassaignolles)	6th Dragoons 6th Cuirassiers
Chief Engineer (Bizot)	

Russian Orders of Battle

(from *Hodasevich*)

RUSSIAN ARMY AT THE ALMA

Army HQ (Prince Menshikov)

16th Division
(Kvetinski)
	1st Bde Vladimir Regiment
	           Susdal Regiment
	2nd Bde Uglitz Regiment
	           Kazan Regiment
	16th Artillery Bde 2 light batteries
	                        1 heavy battery

17th Division
(Kiriakov)
	1st Bde Moscow Regiment
	2nd Bde Borodino Regiment
	           Tarutin Regiment
	17th Artillery Bde 2 light batteries
	                        1 heavy battery

14th Division (Gorchakov)	1st Bde Volhynia Regiment Minsk Regiment
Additional troops	6th Rifle Battalion 4 reserve bns Brest–Bialystok Regt (from 13th Div) 2 battalions sailors, with 4 guns
Cavalry	2 Sqdns Hussars (outpost line) 2 Sotnias Cossacks 2 Regiments Hussars 2 Regiments Don Cossacks 2 Horse Artillery batteries.

RUSSIAN ARMY AT INKERMAN

SOIMONOV'S ARMY (19,000 men, 38 guns)

10th Division	1st Bde Katerinburg Regiment
	2nd Bde Tomsk Regiment
	Kolivansk Regiment
16th Division	1st Bde Vladimir Regiment
	Susdal Regiment
	2nd Bde Uglitz Regiment
17th Division	1st Bde Butirsk Regiment

PAULOV'S ARMY (16,000 men, 96 guns)

11th Division	1st Bde Selinghinsk Regiment
	Yakutsk Regiment
	2nd Bde Okhotsk Regiment
17th Division	2nd Bde Borodino Regiment
	Tarutin Regiment

GORCHAKOV'S ARMY (Balaclava front) 20,000 men, 88 guns
No details

RUSSIAN ARMY AT THE BATTLE OF CHERNAYA
(from *Sir Eveyln Wood*)

Army HQ (Gorchakov)

Right Wing (General Read) 2,000 Cavalry, 13,000 infantry,
62 guns
7th Division
12th Division

Left Wing (General Liprandi) 16,000 infantry, 70 guns
6th Division
12th Division

Reserve
4th Division
5th Division

Notes on Artillery in the Crimea

British guns used in the Crimea were as follows:

FIELD ARTILLERY

Weight of shell	calibre	overall weight behind gun teams	maximum range
6 pr	3·6″	27 cwt	600 yds
9 pr	4·2″	38 cwt	800 yds
12 pr howitzer	4·5″	29 cwt	1000 yds
24 pr ,,	5·7″	38 cwt	1025 yds

Types of ammunition used—shot, common shell, shrapnel (up to maximum range); case shot and carcasses (incendiaries) (range up to about 350 yards).

CONGREVE ROCKETS

6 pr	600 yds
12 pr	1000 yds

POSITION ARTILLERY

12 pr	4·6″	44 cwt	1000 yds
18 pr	5·2″	65 cwt	2000 yds
32 pr howitzer	6·3″	46 cwt	1400 yds
8 inch ,,	8″	54 cwt	1700 yds

SIEGE ARTILLERY

8″ and 10″ guns and howitzers	2000 yds

32 pr	2900 yds
68 pr	2600 yds
Lancaster gun	

MORTARS

8″	1720 yds
10″	2530 yds
13″	2700 yds

Mortars were fired at a fixed elevation of 45°, the range being varied by altering the charge. Once the range was found, they could be fired repeatedly without being relaid. For this reason they were mainly kept for night firing, while the day bombardment was carried out by the 'horizontal fire' of the guns.

Index